OUR WORLD

Learn Italian with Puzzles

Italian Language Learning Puzzle Book (Vol 3)

Play Italian

Book Cover by Adam Guballa

Books by Play Italian

- Travel to Italy – Learn Italian with Puzzles

- Home and Family – Learn Italian with Puzzles

- Our World – Learn Italian with Puzzles

HOW TO USE THIS BOOK

Thank you for buying a copy of *Our World*, the third in a series of puzzle books aimed at Italian language students. The idea is to have fun while you pick up some new Italian vocabulary, specifically related to life on our beautiful planet Earth.

For instance, you'll be able to pick up new words about the natural world: animals, plants, the environment, geography, mountains and oceans, as well as some words related to current themes, such as climate change.

This book includes:

- 30 word searches
- 18 freeform crosswords
- 15 word fit puzzles
- 14 word matches
- 11 word scrambles
- 12 cryptograms

The puzzles are designed to help beginners pick up new words, or intermediate students to brush up their Italian knowledge. As I wanted the puzzles to be fun and challenging for both levels, I have structured the book the following way:

Word Searches

The word searches have Italian words that you need to find in the grid. Words can go in any direction: left to right, right to left, top to bottom, bottom to top, diagonally up or down.

The majority of word searches comes in two versions: *a* and *b*.

Version *a*, the more challenging one (ideal for intermediate students), has the words in Italian inside the grid, but in English below the grid. This means that you have to translate the English words into Italian first, before finding them within the grid. Version *b*, (ideal for beginner students) has the words in Italian both inside the grid and below the grid.

For extra fun, even though version *b* has the same Italian words inside the grid as version *a*, these word are located in different places within the grid, so it will feel like you're solving two different puzzles.

Freeform Crosswords

The freeform crosswords have the clues in Italian, but there is also a Help section in the book, on page 128, with the clues in English, for those who struggle to understand the Italian clues. The clues in English are not necessarily a literal translation of the Italian clues.

Word Fit Puzzles

These can work well for both beginners and intermediate students, as it's about placing the words correctly within the grid.
I recommend you start with letter sizes that have the fewest words. So if there are only 2 words with 5 letters and 6 words with 4 letters, try placing the 5 letter words first.

Word Scrambles

These are lists of words that have been scrambled, and your task is to place the letters in the correct order. As these can be particularly challenging, they are designed in two varieties: an easier one, where some letters are suggested, and a trickier one, with no help.

Cryptograms

These are usually quotes from someone famous. To stay within this book's overall theme, the quotes are related to the topic of our natural world.

Your task is to replace the numbers in the puzzle with the correct letters, and reveal the quote.

For these you have the option of using some of the hints provided, or just try to complete the activity without the help.

These may be easier to complete for a student of Italian at intermediate level, but even if you're a beginner, why not try?

Word Matches

These come in two types. The first one is about matching Italian words to English words, so it's a straightforward translation activity. The second one is about matching Italian words to other Italian words (by context). The latter is probably more suitable for intermediate level students, but again, if you're a beginner, it's worth a try, perhaps with the help of an Italian dictionary.

Solutions

All solutions are provided at the end of the book. For easier reference, the solutions are grouped by puzzle type. So you will find all the word search solutions first, then all the crossword solutions, and so on.

And finally…

A little about me. My name is Martina and I was born and brought up in Italy. I am passionate about languages, and having fun while learning.

This is the third puzzle book I created for Italian language learners.

I also have a website with plenty of resources, puzzles and games. Some you can download, print and solve at home, some you can play online. You can also subscribe to my monthly newsletter and receive free puzzles and fun Italian learning resources.

Go on… have a look at *playitalian.com* and do let me know how you get on.

Ciao for now

Martina

Martina

Alcuni alberi

Translate the English words below the grid into Italian and find them in the Word Search. If this is too challenging, please turn the page for an easier puzzle.

```
E B F Y S S G N Y O I C C E L
T U E P N R P Y O D P O E E N
E U C S G A R G R X N P E U P
B C I A L L U T E B A B O A B
A P L M L R G W C O X O N I P
T E A O N I S S A R F K A C P
K O S S E R P I C D O V T A Z
C N S L C R N T U E C O N C X
I G Y R I F S C O C P M O A N
V A I C R E U Q I N I L I L O
O T Y Q A L J Y L G A O G U B
J S K T L U Y Y G T D T G Z U
G A L Z J X H E I X M O A T H
F C J E C Z Z X T J R I F L N
K S S N G Y F X G T J L O A P
```

FIR TREE	EUCALYPTUS	ALDER
ACACIA	BEECH	PALM
MAPLE	ASH	PINE
BAOBAB	MULBERRY	POPLAR
BIRCH	LARCH	PLANE-TREE
CHESTNUT	ELM	OAK
CEDAR	HOLM-OAK	WILLOW
CYPRESS	WALNUT	LIME TREE

Alcuni alberi

Find the Italian words below the grid in the Word Search puzzle. These are the same Italian words as in 1a, but they're located in different positions on the grid.

```
R H R U U P B K A N Y R O K N
F E C Z D O P P O I P F C O V
E U C A L I P T O I R C L V M
C P Q O N G A T S A C M X N A
I M P N N G H L S L O C A B M
L K S A W A A S E L R P E C L
A O V T C F I Y R U D T Z L A
S N T A N N C C P T E Y K F P
V X C L O J R L I E C I R A L
A I M P N P E M C B E E C D R
A O X L A G U N Q A E E R Q Q
Z K H D T V Q P B B R Y M S N
H R R O N I P Y A O I L G I T
A X D K O S L E G A K X L D K
B B N A L T S O E B X Y D X Q
```

ABETE
ACACIA
ACERO
BAOBAB
BETULLA
CASTAGNO
CEDRO
CIPRESSO

EUCALIPTO
FAGGIO
FRASSINO
GELSO
LARICE
OLMO
LECCIO
NOCE

ONTANO
PALMA
PINO
PIOPPO
PLATANO
QUERCIA
SALICE
TIGLIO

Alcuni mammiferi

Translate the English words below the grid into Italian and find them in the Word Search. If this is too challenging, please turn the page for an easier puzzle.

```
F  P  J  Y  R  K  P  U  Z  Z  O  L  A  H  S
K  O  M  A  T  O  P  O  P  P  I  A  P  C  K
T  I  R  F  U  R  E  T  T  O  X  V  I  A  E
A  R  U  M  A  C  O  F  I  B  R  M  T  V  V
B  A  F  L  I  P  J  K  V  C  M  U  G  A  Q
V  D  C  A  O  C  E  H  C  I  R  T  E  L  P
D  E  W  L  L  E  H  Y  A  K  J  P  L  L  U
A  M  A  L  O  T  S  I  Q  B  E  A  A  O  J
A  O  T  E  T  N  O  R  E  C  O  N  I  R  H
I  R  W  Z  T  O  S  R  O  R  T  N  H  B  C
I  D  A  Z  A  S  J  R  H  I  E  E  G  V  E
N  D  P  A  I  I  A  H  L  O  C  R  N  F  P
U  Z  O  G  O  B  E  O  T  Y  I  G  I  P  L
O  J  B  R  C  O  P  I  D  A  R  B  C  L  A
L  C  C  Z  S  E  R  P  E  L  C  B  R  Y  P
```

MOOSE	SEAL	SHEEP
ANTELOPE	ANTEATER	SKUNK
BISON	FERRET	REINDEER
SLOTH	GAZELLE	RHINO
HAMSTER	HIPPO	MONKEY
HORSE	LAMA	SQUIRREL
WILD BOAR	HARE	MOUSE
DROMEDARY	BEAR	WALRUS

Alcuni mammiferi

Find the Italian words below the grid in the Word Search puzzle. These are the same Italian words as in 2a, but they're located in different positions on the grid.

```
V P H O P O T X B U C Q S A F
U O A L O Z Z U P R X C U O S
E P O L I T N A I S O Q C C E
Z I C A L P I C N I G A I L C
P D E V O E E T A J K M E F M
G A H A J T Z T Q W M A T M Z
Q R C C O N T Z D I Y L N A D
O B I E M O I R A D E M O R D
H H R I L R F A F G Y G S O S
I V T O L E L A I H G N I C L
F O R M I C H I E R E O B E L
T S F A E O M A T O P O P P I
O N O R A N N E R O E R T K G
X G R O W I Q F Z B E Y U H G
O O T T E R U F D L Z T Y N F
```

ALCE	FOCA	PECORA
ANTILOPE	FORMICHIERE	PUZZOLA
BISONTE	FURETTO	RENNA
BRADIPO	GAZZELLA	RINOCERONTE
CRICETO	IPPOPOTAMO	SCIMMIA
CAVALLO	LAMA	SCOIATTOLO
CINGHIALE	LEPRE	TOPO
DROMEDARIO	ORSO	TRICHECO

Insetti antipatici

This freeform crossword has the clues in Italian. If you struggle to understand some of the clues, you can find them in English in the *Help Section* on page 128

Orizzontali

4. Fastidioso parassita dei capelli
7. Parassiti che attaccano le piante
9. Assomiglia all'ape ma non fa miele
11. La sua puntura è molto dolorosa
12. Insetto piccolissimo che vola

Verticali

1. Può vivere nel letto e succhia il sangue
2. Gli piace mangiare il legno
3. Ha lunghe antenne e viene anche chiamato blatta
5. Una cavalletta che distrugge
6. Può causare la malaria
8. Tormenta cani e gatti
10. Piccolo insetto alato, di solito nero

Disastri naturali

This freeform crossword has the clues in Italian. If you struggle to understand some of the clues, you can find them in English in the *Help Section* on page 128

Orizzontali

1. Sisma del fondo marino

6. Cola dal vulcano in eruzione

8. Enorme massa di neve che rotola giù

9. Periodo prolungato senza pioggia

10. Quando la terra trema sotto i piedi

11. Fuoco violento che distrugge

Verticali

2. La causa dell'estinzione dei dinosauri

3. Si chiamava Katrina quello di New Orleans del 2005

4. Un vortice d'aria molto violento

5. Preoccupava Noè quando costruiva l'arca

7. Caduta di terra e rocce lungo la montagna

Uccelli rapaci

Match the Italian words on the left, to the English words on the right.

aquila	merlin
falco	sparrowhawk
nibbio	kestrel
avvoltoio	kite
gufo	eagle
condor	buzzard
gheppio	hawk
poiana	harrier
albanella	condor
barbagianni	vulture
sparviero	owl
smeriglio	barn owl

Stagioni: inverno

Match the Italian words on the left, to the English words on the right.

pozzanghera	cold
brina	December
neve	hybernation
raffreddore	fir tree
buio	snow
letargo	artichoke
freddo	frost
dicembre	darkness
arancia	puddle
carciofo	cold
finocchio	orange
abete	fennel

Il mondo dei felini

Below this Word Fit puzzle there is a list of words.
Place the words correctly into the grid.

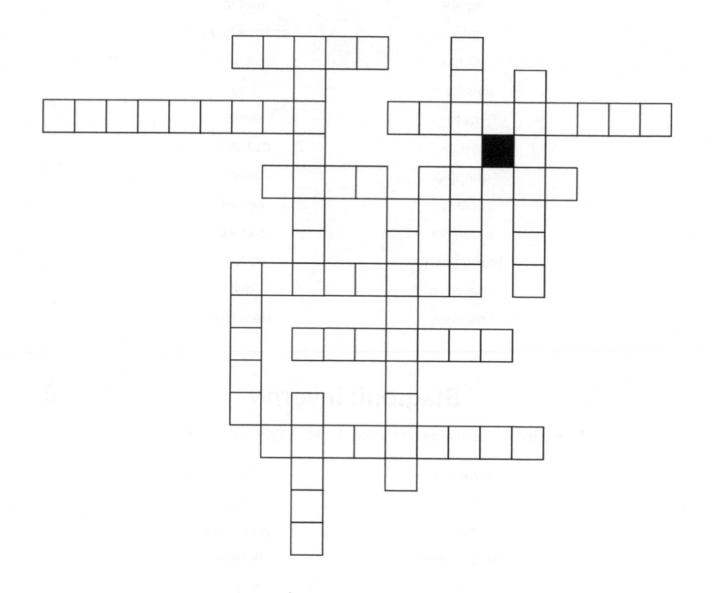

4 lettere	**7 lettere**	**8 lettere**	**9 lettere**
Puma	Artigli	Ghepardo	Carnivoro
	Pantera	Giaguaro	Destrezza
5 lettere		Leopardo	Pelliccia
Gatto			Predatore
Leone			
Lince			
Tigre			

Cose del deserto

The following words have been scrambled. Place the letters in the correct order.
For a less challenging version of this puzzle, please turn the page.

ECMAOLML   _ _ _ _ _ _ _ _

POOICSENR   _ _ _ _ _ _ _ __

ABISAB   _ _ _ _ _ _

UAND   _ _ _ _

AISO   _ _ _ _

ATUSCC   _ _ _ _ _ _

IZLNSOIE   _ _ _ _ _ _ _ _

OAIRMGIG   _ _ _ _ _ _ _ _

ETOVN   _ _ _ _ _

EVELROP   _ _ _ _ _ _ _

STPAEMET   _ _ _ _ _ _ _ _

COAIRC   _ _ _ _ _ _

Cose del deserto

The words on the left have been scrambled. Place the letters in the correct order.

ECMAOLML   C _ _ M _ _ _ O

POOICSENR   S _ _ _ P _ _ _ E

ABISAB   S _ _ _ _ A

UAND   D _ _ _

AISO   _ A _ _

ATUSCC   C _ _ T _ _

IZLNSOIE   S _ _ _ N _ _ O

OAIRMGIG   M _ _ _ _ _ _ O

ETOVN   V _ _ _ _

EVELROP   P _ _ _ _ _ E

STPAEMET   T _ _ P _ _ _ A

COAIRC   R _ _ _ _ _

Quote by Ralph Waldo Emerson

Replace the numbers in the grid with the correct letters, and reveal the quote.

Hints: 30 = A   5 = G   19 = I   33 = L   24 = T

| 7 | 5 | 18 | 19 |

| 26 | 30 | 1 | 24 | 19 | 8 | 7 | 33 | 30 | 1 | 25 |

| 19 | 18 |

| 18 | 30 | 24 | 32 | 1 | 30 |

| 32 | 18 | 30 |

| 22 | 7 | 5 | 33 | 19 | 30 |

| 32 | 18 | 30 |

| 5 | 7 | 8 | 8 | 19 | 30 |

| 32 | 18 |

| 8 | 1 | 19 | 31 | 24 | 30 | 33 | 33 | 7 |

| 32 | 18 |

| 10 | 7 | 10 | 25 | 18 | 24 | 7 |

| 28 | 25 | 33 |

| 24 | 25 | 10 | 26 | 7 |

| 3 |

| 33 | 25 | 5 | 30 | 24 | 7 |

| 30 | 33 |

| 24 | 32 | 24 | 24 | 7 |

| 25 |

| 26 | 30 | 1 | 24 | 25 | 8 | 19 | 26 | 30 |

| 28 | 25 | 33 | 33 | 30 |

| 26 | 25 | 1 | 22 | 25 | 11 | 19 | 7 | 18 | 25 |

| 28 | 25 | 33 |

| 24 | 32 | 24 | 24 | 7 |

Quote by Cristoforo Colombo

Replace the numbers in the grid with the correct letters, and reveal the quote.

Hints: 7 = C   32 = E   21 = I   24 = M

| 20 | 21 | 7 | 30 |

| 7 | 22 | 32 |

| 21 | 16 |

| 24 | 30 | 28 | 20 | 30 |

| 28 | 30 | 28 |

| 8 |

| 7 | 30 | 9 | 25 |

| 1 | 13 | 12 | 28 | 20 | 32 |

| 7 | 30 | 24 | 32 |

| 16 | 30 |

| 27 | 13 | 32 | 4 | 32 | 28 | 20 | 32 |

| 16 | 12 |

| 1 | 32 | 28 | 4 | 32 |

Cose del mare

Below this Word Fit puzzle there is a list of words.
Place the words correctly into the grid.

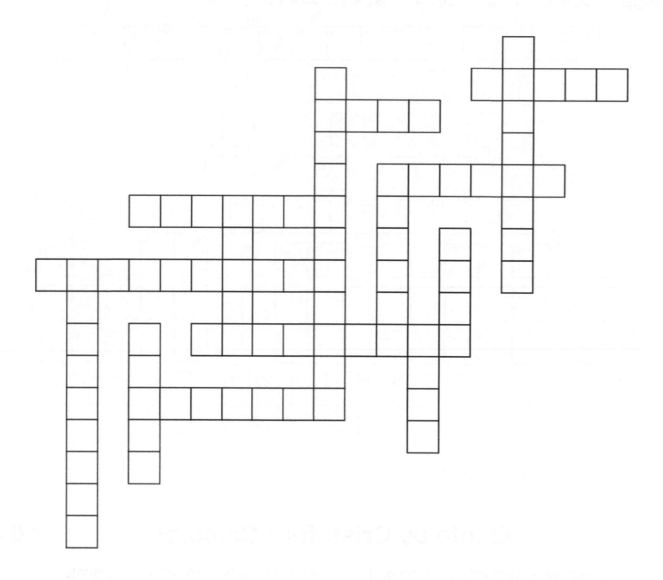

4 lettere
Faro
Nave
Onda

5 lettere
Alghe
Barca
Marea

6 lettere
Sabbia
Sirena

7 lettere
Corallo
Relitto

8 lettere
Gabbiano

9 lettere
Orizzonte
Pellicano

10 lettere
Conchiglia

11 lettere
Sottomarino

Animali notturni

Translate the English words below the grid into Italian and find them in the Word Search. If this is too challenging, please turn the page for an easier puzzle.

```
E  P  L  O  V  O  O  F  U  G  X  Z  P  F  S
O  N  I  P  S  O  C  R  O  P  P  C  L  F  M
L  Y  N  P  F  I  E  G  J  X  J  E  B  P  Q
L  E  L  A  I  H  G  N  I  C  O  N  P  N  F
A  T  E  C  O  S  S  A  T  P  I  O  P  U  L
C  O  Z  O  R  O  T  S  A  C  C  I  M  M  L
A  Y  F  R  I  O  V  R  E  C  C  C  R  V  W
I  O  P  U  H  L  D  D  E  E  I  O  U  J  T
C  C  Z  G  G  O  T  U  X  L  R  R  F  Z  T
S  X  U  N  E  R  P  E  L  I  L  P  R  H  H
M  Y  J  A  R  A  Z  N  A  Z  T  O  K  D  T
C  Q  T  C  G  P  H  H  N  R  I  T  S  V  F
T  O  S  V  I  L  R  W  E  T  H  T  Z  D  F
P  R  D  N  T  A  J  O  I  K  R  A  M  U  P
C  J  T  R  P  T  Q  I  Z  M  Q  R  N  Q  B
```

KANGAROO	HYENA	RAT
BEAVER	LEOPARD	HEDGEHOG
DEER	HARE	JACKAL
WILD BOAR	WOLF	MOLE
COYOTE	BAT	BADGER
GECKO	PORCUPINE	TIGER
DORMOUSE	RACCOON	FOX
OWL	PUMA	MOSQUITO

12b   Animali notturni

Find the Italian words below the grid in the Word Search puzzle. These are the same Italian words as in 12a, but they're located in different positions on the grid.

```
D  R  N  B  W  M  P  J  C  G  Z  T  Y  H  S
A  O  T  T  A  R  T  E  G  E  A  N  E  I  D
P  I  P  I  S  T  R  E  L  L  O  P  U  L  H
L  C  N  X  L  V  O  L  P  P  N  S  W  Y  D
R  C  W  E  O  L  L  A  C  A  I  C  S  G  C
K  I  P  R  D  C  K  I  G  T  P  U  U  A  N
J  R  I  G  R  B  E  H  P  O  S  F  V  M  T
E  M  C  I  A  V  I  G  E  H  O  L  H  U  G
P  A  X  T  P  R  E  N  O  I  C  O  R  P  P
L  Y  W  S  O  G  T  I  R  R  R  C  X  E  X
O  I  X  N  E  E  O  C  U  O  O  N  N  X  M
V  K  Y  D  L  N  Y  S  G  Q  P  T  A  U  T
L  O  M  V  L  W  O  E  N  V  M  W  S  C  H
G  K  W  S  F  Y  C  Z  A  R  A  Z  N  A  Z
X  G  Q  T  N  V  W  B  C  T  B  F  G  R  C
```

CANGURO	IENA	RATTO
CASTORO	LEOPARDO	RICCIO
CERVO	LEPRE	SCIACALLO
CINGHIALE	LUPO	TALPA
COYOTE	PIPISTRELLO	TASSO
GECO	PORCOSPINO	TIGRE
GHIRO	PROCIONE	VOLPE
GUFO	PUMA	ZANZARA

Alcuni Stati del mondo

Translate the English words below the grid into Italian and find them in the Word Search. If this is too challenging, please turn the page for an easier puzzle.

```
F A O Q A I N O T S E U Y P C
A I R A G L U B U F Y N V L J
A I H C R U T D E A N G A P S
F Q E R O P A G N I S H I A V
O I T A Q F A O O G A E D I F
I N L M R N Z I P E M R N R U
W Z A I C E R G P V G I I T Z
O B C N P A R L A R K A N S I
C A A A A P M E I O K W X U M
Q I N D I M I B G N O K F A O
F Z I P C A I N O T T E L I U
F A A I N A M R E G I D T L Q
A O R C A A R E Z Z I V S A S
M R C O R E D S C V Z A Z T H
J C U S F G I F E R F D D I P
```

AUSTRIA	FRANCE	NORWAY
BELGIUM	GERMANY	SINGAPORE
BULGARIA	JAPAN	SPAIN
CAMBODIA	GREECE	SOUTH AFRICA
CROATIA	INDIA	SWITZERLAND
DENMARK	ITALY	TURKEY
ESTONIA	LATVIA	UKRAINE
PHILIPPINES	MALDIVES	HUNGARY

Alcuni Stati del mondo

Find the Italian words below the grid in the Word Search puzzle. These are the same Italian words as in 13a, but they're located in different positions on the grid.

```
A  I  R  T  S  U  A  R  E  Z  Z  I  V  S  F
I  V  H  V  W  A  Y  N  R  U  I  H  B  K  R
H  C  Y  S  V  A  I  G  O  B  M  A  C  S  A
C  I  C  O  Y  P  X  R  P  F  O  W  F  X  N
R  N  U  V  P  A  C  R  A  M  I  N  A  D  C
U  B  F  I  A  C  V  C  G  G  G  T  Z  R  I
T  A  L  U  E  I  G  K  N  S  L  Q  X  Q  A
A  I  G  E  V  R  O  N  I  N  E  U  Y  Q  N
F  N  D  N  I  F  A  O  S  Q  B  F  B  C  I
G  A  U  O  D  A  I  N  O  T  T  E  L  R  A
R  M  H  P  L  D  E  S  T  O  N  I  A  O  R
E  R  T  P  A  U  I  T  A  L  I  A  I  A  C
C  E  V  A  M  S  P  Z  C  X  I  D  D  Z  U
I  G  A  I  R  E  H  G  N  U  Y  G  N  I  C
A  A  N  G  A  P  S  A  P  Z  E  T  I  A  D
```

AUSTRIA	FRANCIA	NORVEGIA
BELGIO	GERMANIA	SINGAPORE
BULGARIA	GIAPPONE	SPAGNA
CAMBOGIA	GRECIA	SUDAFRICA
CROAZIA	INDIA	SVIZZERA
DANIMARCA	ITALIA	TURCHIA
ESTONIA	LETTONIA	UCRAINA
FILIPPINE	MALDIVE	UNGHERIA

L'Universo e lo Spazio

Translate the English words below the grid into Italian and find them in the Word Search. If this is too challenging, please turn the page for an easier puzzle.

```
O  O  I  R  U  C  R  E  M  O  N  A  R  U  M
N  N  S  T  O  O  V  A  T  I  B  R  O  A  Y
R  U  N  M  T  S  D  W  M  P  A  R  R  F  H
U  T  E  G  A  T  U  A  N  O  R  T  S  A  F
T  T  R  O  I  E  V  N  N  C  E  R  A  Z  S
A  E  E  M  M  L  E  U  T  S  F  E  I  H  E
S  N  N  U  O  L  C  L  E  E  S  T  S  O  P
A  B  E  V  N  A  I  G  O  L  O  M  S  O  C
T  E  V  L  O  Z  R  M  C  E  M  Y  A  A  N
E  A  N  J  R  I  A  O  M  T  T  Q  L  T  O
L  L  H  U  T  O  H  A  E  A  A  I  A  E  V
L  L  O  G  S  N  K  N  Z  T  Q  Q  G  N  J
I  E  Y  S  A  E  D  I  O  R  E  T  S  A  B
T  T  S  S  D  P  F  K  A  D  I  M  L  I  S
E  S  S  I  L  C  E  N  O  T  U  L  P  P  L
```

ASTEROID	GALAXY	PLUTO
ASTRONOMY	MOON	SATELLITE
ASTRONAUT	MARS	SATURN
ATMOSPHERE	MERCURY	SUN
COMET	METEOR	STAR
COSMOLOGY	NEPTUNE	TELESCOPE
CONSTELLATION	ORBIT	URANUS
ECLIPSE	PLANET	VENUS

L'Universo e lo Spazio

Find the Italian words below the grid in the Word Search puzzle. These are the same Italian words as in 14a, but they're located in different positions on the grid.

```
W  G  T  G  Y  X  W  N  U  Z  W  H  S  X  A
W  A  T  U  A  N  O  R  T  S  A  B  O  P  T
Y  T  I  G  B  Z  A  G  Z  Y  X  U  N  Y  E
H  E  W  G  P  N  C  K  O  N  U  T  T  E  N
H  M  S  F  O  I  R  U  C  R  E  M  A  T  A
C  O  S  T  E  L  L  A  Z  I  O  N  E  I  I
S  C  S  U  Z  R  O  I  X  J  U  L  D  L  P
A  A  R  E  F  S  O  M  T  A  E  E  I  L  A
T  I  A  N  H  E  L  O  S  S  L  R  O  E  S
U  S  A  O  V  O  D  N  C  O  F  E  R  T  B
R  S  A  T  I  B  R  O  P  G  C  N  E  A  V
N  A  N  U  L  J  P  R  A  L  L  E  T  S  D
O  L  K  L  X  I  E  T  R  A  M  V  S  F  C
G  A  F  P  O  E  S  S  I  L  C  E  A  I  Q
E  G  V  N  W  D  G  A  R  O  E  T  E  M  J
```

ASTEROIDE	GALASSIA	PLUTONE
ASTRONOMIA	LUNA	SATELLITE
ASTRONAUTA	MARTE	SATURNO
ATMOSFERA	MERCURIO	SOLE
COMETA	METEORA	STELLA
COSMOLOGIA	NETTUNO	TELESCOPIO
COSTELLAZIONE	ORBITA	URANO
ECLISSE	PIANETA	VENERE

Animali carnivori

This freeform crossword has the clues in Italian. If you struggle to understand some of the clues, you can find them in English in the *Help Section* on page 128

Orizzontali

2. Fa impaurire le pecore
6. Saltella e vive nello stagno
7. Enorme serpente che stritola
9. Tesse la tela
11. Il re della foresta
12. Uccello che si nutre di animali morti

Verticali

1. Enorme rettile con forti mandibole
3. Un felino domestico
4. Un enorme cetaceo
5. Uccello che vive in Antartide
8. Un rapace dal volo agile e maestoso
10. Feroce predatore marino

16 **Animali erbivori**

16

Animali erbivori

This freeform crossword has the clues in Italian. If you struggle to understand some of the clues, you can find them in English in the *Help Section* on page 129

Orizzontali

6. Quadrupede con collo lunghissimo

7. Animale da fattoria con la barbetta

8. Vive nel deserto e beve tanta acqua

10. Animale enorme con una lunga proboscide

11. Animaletto peloso con le orecchie lunghe

Verticali

1. Produce il latte più bevuto

2. La scimmia più grande

3. Ha le strisce bianche e nere

4. Quello di Troia era di legno

5. Rettile che cammina lentamente

8. Ruminante con grandi corna

9. Animale da soma un po' testardo

20

Animali che vanno in letargo

Match the Italian words on the left, to the English words on the right.

pipistrello	squirrel
orso	bat
ghiro	raccoon
bombo	marmot
rana	snake
scoiattolo	hedgehog
riccio	frog
lucertola	bumblebee
marmotta	toad
procione	dormouse
serpente	lizard
rospo	bear

Stagioni: primavera

Match the Italian words on the left, to the English words on the right.

bocciolo	chick
agnello	bud
nido	meadow
germoglio	pollen
polline	butterfly
risveglio	shoot
allergie	nest
pulcino	March
erba	lamb
marzo	awakening
prato	grass
farfalla	allergies

Salviamo il pianeta

Below this Word Fit puzzle there is a list of words.
Place the words correctly into the grid.

7 lettere
Governi
Impatto
Impegno
Risorse

8 lettere
Ecologia
Rispetto

11 lettere
Prevenzione
Riciclaggio
Rinnovabili

12 lettere
Salvaguardia

14 lettere
Responsabilità
Rimboschimento

Polo Nord e Polo Sud

Below this Word Fit puzzle there is a list of words.
Place the words correctly into the grid.

4 lettere
Neve
Foca

5 lettere
Renna

6 lettere
Artide
Bufera
Freddo

7 lettere
Narvalo
Iceberg

8 lettere
Ghiaccio
Pinguino
Tricheco

9 lettere
Antartide
Sottozero

10 lettere
Spedizione

11 lettere
Esploratore

Quote by G.K. Chesterton

Replace the numbers in the grid with the correct letters, and reveal the quote.

Hints: 5 = B   4 = E   9 = L   11 = 0   29 = U

Row 1: [4] | [31] [29] [6] [25] [10] [11] | [30] [14] [11] [3] [4]

Row 2: [26] [29] [9] [9] [6] | [2] [29] [6]

Row 3: [26] [19] [14] [9] [6] [2] [6] | [12] [29] [6] [28] [10] [6]

Row 4: [14] [25] | [6] [9] [2] [11] | [30] [14] [29] [2] [2] [11] [26] [2] [11]

Row 5: [18] [17] [4] | [14] [25] | [5] [6] [26] [26] [11]

Row 6: [26] [4] [25] [22] [6] | [9] [6] | [30] [14] [11] [12] [12] [14] [6]

Row 7: [25] [11] [25] | [18] [14] | [26] [6] [28] [4] [5] [5] [4]

Row 8: [6] [28] [18] [11] [5] [6] [9] [4] [25] [11]

Quote by Marco Aurelio

Replace the numbers in the grid with the correct letters, and reveal the quote.

Hints: 16 = E   24 = N   4 = T   30 = U

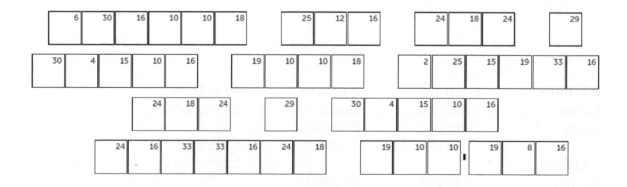

Erbe aromatiche

The following words have been scrambled. Place the letters in the correct order.
For a less challenging version of this puzzle, please turn the page.

NTLBELIEA   _ _ _ _ _ _ _ _ _

ZINEDIDAO   _ _ _ _ _ _ _ _ _

IVNIOIDES   _ _ _ _ _ _ _ _ _

OEISATTONRZ   _ _ _ _ _ _ _ _ _ _ _

RNPECAETLUE   _ _ _ _ _ _ _ _ _ _ _

ZENAROIF   _ _ _ _ _ _ _ _

AEMCIDIL   _ _ _ _ _ _ _ _

TMIIECARAT   _ _ _ _ _ _ _ _ _ _

UOMERN   _ _ _ _ _ _

UASIRM   _ _ _ _ _ _

ILTLMOUP   _ _ _ _ _ _ _ _

OTGEAERIM   _ _ _ _ _ _ _ _ _

Erbe aromatiche

The words on the left have been scrambled. Place the letters in the correct order.

OAOLRL   A _ _ _ _ O

OETAN   A _ _ _ _

ILACBOSI   B _ _ _ _ _ O

DOAIROOCLN C _ _ _ N _ _ _ O

NOGCOLLAEDR D _ _ _ _ _ C _ _ _O

GAAMRAGONI M _ _ _ I _ _ _ _ A

NEMAT   M _ _ _ _

RGONOIA   O _ _ _ _ _ O

ZMOREOLPEZ P _ _ _ _ _ _ _ _ _ O

ARMOINSRO   R _ _ _ A _ _ _ O

AVAILS   S _ _ _ _ _

OTIM   T _ _ _

Alcuni uccelli

Translate the English words below the grid into Italian and find them in the Word Search. If this is too challenging, please turn the page for an easier puzzle.

```
M H F D X E M I B B S K K O C
E Q E N O I C C I P O E J Z U
R O N A I B B A G O O K F Z C
L A I H C C A N R O C D E U U
O R C H L S P Y E P I T N R L
U T O L L A G A P P A P O T O
D A T N S N D F E G P N V S L
A N T S I I T S M K D Q A P L
B A E U O L O N G I S U P V A
M R R Q I L L A N G O C I C G
O B O M H A H E N O R I A R B
L O C S C G S C D N W K Z Z W
O N G I C O S S O R I T T E P
C A I A I L G A U Q A G P H E
M H P P P V B O N I H C C A T
```

HERON	FLAMINGO	ROBIN
DUCK	SEAGULL	WOODPECKER
GOLDFINCH	HEN	PIGEON
STORK	ROOSTER	QUAIL
SWAN	BLACKBIRD	SWALLOW
DOVE	PARROT	OSTRICH
CROW	SPARROW	TURKEY
CUCKOO	PEACOCK	NIGHTINGALE

Alcuni uccelli

Find the Italian words below the grid in the Word Search puzzle. These are the same Italian words as in 24a, but they're located in different positions on the grid.

```
H T Z G H B R O E N O V A P X
P A P P A G A L L O N G I C T
G R V M U N O L R E M Y L N U
V T U L X O N A I B B A G F M
Q A S O A T S G W N A C A O F
E N O R I A T S Y R V G U L H
A A E O H A N G O C I C Q U F
F E N I C O T T E R O V S C H
O N I H C C A T G Z I I D U D
R O D C A N I L L A G T U C N
E I N C N J Y S F N H H T C C
S C O I R A B M O L O C G E J
S C R P O N I L L E D R A C P
A I O S C H O Z Z U R T S V K
P P S E Q S W V C H M U O P Q
```

AIRONE	FENICOTTERO	PETTIROSSO
ANATRA	GABBIANO	PICCHIO
CARDELLINO	GALLINA	PICCIONE
CICOGNA	GALLO	QUAGLIA
CIGNO	MERLO	RONDINE
COLOMBA	PAPPAGALLO	STRUZZO
CORNACCHIA	PASSERO	TACCHINO
CUCULO	PAVONE	USIGNOLO

Metalli e leghe

Translate the English words below the grid into Italian and find them in the Word Search. If this is too challenging, please turn the page for an easier puzzle.

```
I  T  M  P  D  I  O  Z  N  O  R  B  M  E  Y
G  R  U  B  N  T  O  B  M  O  I  P  S  I  A
O  Z  L  F  T  A  N  E  O  I  R  A  B  P  K
A  S  C  O  I  A  I  C  C  A  X  T  R  I  F
M  L  N  I  O  S  T  J  S  L  Z  C  L  W  B
A  E  L  R  M  I  A  O  N  G  A  T  S  E  Z
G  H  O  U  Z  H  L  X  Y  R  H  M  U  M  P
L  C  I  C  M  G  P  O  G  P  O  R  R  E  F
A  I  O  R  O  I  S  E  N  G  A  M  L  M  E
M  N  Q  E  S  E  N  A  G  N  A  M  O  A  D
A  H  O  M  W  T  E  I  I  K  G  P  N  R  O
Q  O  I  D  O  R  B  O  O  T  L  A  B  O  C
C  L  I  C  T  G  E  M  N  L  R  B  G  R  N
D  F  P  P  C  S  T  J  S  P  D  K  F  R  I
R  G  K  B  J  W  V  V  E  K  O  I  K  Z  Z
```

STEEL	IRON	PEWTER
SILVER	CAST IRON	PLATINUM
ALUMINIUM	MAGNESIUM	LEAD
AMALGAM	MANGANESE	COPPER
BARIUM	MERCURY	RHODIUM
BRONZE	NICKEL	TIN
COBALT	GOLD	URANIUM
CHROMIUM	BRASS	ZINC

Metalli e leghe

Find the Italian words below the grid in the Word Search puzzle. These are the same Italian words as in 25a, but they're located in different positions on the grid.

```
R  J  D  U  U  T  Q  V  O  Z  N  O  R  B  V
G  J  B  N  F  O  O  I  S  E  N  G  A  M  E
X  Q  V  E  S  E  N  A  G  N  A  M  I  P  R
V  J  R  A  O  I  A  I  C  C  A  S  I  H  G
B  R  A  F  M  Q  A  Q  T  L  E  H  C  I  N
O  I  R  U  C  R  E  M  G  A  V  N  S  S  F
T  I  L  Q  G  C  B  A  I  O  L  M  P  V  U
L  L  D  E  O  B  M  O  I  P  G  P  S  R  J
A  N  N  O  Z  A  F  R  F  M  S  L  A  X  S
B  T  R  H  R  I  J  T  C  T  P  N  D  A  A
O  N  G  A  T  S  I  L  N  Q  I  V  W  C  W
C  M  M  H  G  W  A  E  N  O  T  T  O  V  O
Q  E  O  I  R  A  B  P  Q  N  R  B  A  K  D
C  C  U  R  A  N  J  U  R  G  V  O  X  M  V
G  K  V  O  C  N  I  Z  W  E  I  D  Q  K  E
```

ACCIAIO	FERRO	PELTRO
ARGENTO	GHISA	PLATINO
ALLUMINIO	MAGNESIO	PIOMBO
AMALGAMA	MANGANESE	RAME
BARIO	MERCURIO	RODIO
BRONZO	NICHEL	STAGNO
COBALTO	ORO	URANIO
CROMO	OTTONE	ZINCO

Translate the English words below the grid into Italian and find them in the Word Search. If this is too challenging, please turn the page for an easier puzzle.

```
P K C A N A R G A L E M S O V
S E O L L A R O C A S A L A K
D N P L M I T S M O N I V B G
G O R E B M A G A G P F Y Q E
Z P C N R P J A U H W X E O R
U M U I V O R E V A P A P R I
P A L C H A N N G Y Y R A O H
W L N C G J T C A I X V L D T
E E E O I H C C I D A R O O X
Q E S C A I R U G N A O G M T
O T N O M A R T E X O N A O D
A R C C S N F L I H R I R P Z
Y A Q O S Q L V L T B B F Z Z
R M N U R O E N I G G U R F B
A O O F A K M P C Q X R S W N
```

WATERMELON	PRAWN	RED CHICORY
LOBSTER	RASPBERRY	RADISH
CHERRY	MARS	RUBY
LADYBIRD	POMEGRANATE	RUST
CORAL	POPPY	BLOOD
STRAWBERRY	CHILLI	SUNSET
FIRE	TOMATO	WINE

I colori nella natura: Rosso

Find the Italian words below the grid in the Word Search puzzle. These are the same
Italian words as in 26a, but they're located in different positions on the grid.

```
P W Z C N C A K U O L V Z T L
P E N I G G U R A Z I O E L A
S A P R T Z Z G Q N W M U R U
A L L E N I C C O C E E G A C
N O N T R A T F I O A K N T O
A G O R K O U S H W Q G A S P
R A L A W L N O C O U F S O O
G R L M P L B C C R M V M G B
A F A I G E I L I C O O F A C
L O R A D N H A D N D L E R Y
E N O P M A L C A O O T H A V
M I C R Y V O O R E V A P A P
H B U Z L A P O T N O M A R T
E U H Y O R E B M A G G C P U
H R W P I I C N I X S C H P G
```

ANGURIA	GAMBERO	RADICCHIO
ARAGOSTA	LAMPONE	RAVANELLO
CILIEGIA	MARTE	RUBINO
COCCINELLA	MELAGRANA	RUGGINE
CORALLO	PAPAVERO	SANGUE
FRAGOLA	PEPERONCINO	TRAMONTO
FUOCO	POMODORO	VINO

Animali della fattoria

This freeform crossword has the clues in Italian. If you struggle to understand some of the clues, you can find them in English in the *Help Section* on page 129

Orizzontali

3. Da lui vengono i prosciutti
6. Sveglia tutti al mattino
8. Depone un uovo al giorno
9. Ha le orecchie più lunghe del cavallo
11. Uccello messaggero
12. Il miglior amico dell'uomo

Verticali

1. L'uccello che gloglotta
2. Quella nera è rara
4. Segue la mamma chioccia
5. Va a caccia di topi
7. Le sue zampe sono palmate
10. Produce il miele

Fiumi del mondo

This freeform crossword has the clues in Italian. If you struggle to understand some of the clues, you can find them in English in the *Help Section* on page 129

Orizzontali

3. Scorre sotto London Bridge

5. Lunghissimo fiume dell'Europa centrale

7. Il fiume più profondo del mondo

9. Fiume importante d'Egitto

10. Un fiume lunghissimo del Sudamerica

11. Scorre a Parigi

Verticali

1. Importante fiume della Russia

2. Il fiume più lungo degli Stati Uniti

3. Il fiume di Roma

4. Il fiume più lungo d'Italia

6. Scorre sotto il Ponte Vecchio

8. Fiume sacro dell'India

Suoni e natura

Match the Italian words on the left, to the Italian words on the right.

fiume	frusciare
foglie	ronzare
pioggia	scoppiettare
fuoco	battere
fulmine	soffiare
uccelli	eruttare
insetti	cinguettare
cuore	galoppare
cavallo	tuonare
onda del mare	scrosciare
vento	scorrere
vulcano	sciabordare

Animali e cuccioli

Match the Italian words on the left, to the Italian words on the right.

mucca	anatroccolo
cavallo	pulcino
cervo	orsetto
gallina	aquilotto
pecora	puledro
anatra	micetto
aquila	cerbiatto
volpe	vitello
capra	volpacchiotto
gatto	porcellino
maiale	capretto
orso	agnello

Fiori profumati

Below this Word Fit puzzle there is a list of words.
Place the words correctly into the grid.

4 lettere
Rosa

6 lettere
Fresia
Giglio
Peonia

7 lettere
Glicine
Lavanda

8 lettere
Gardenia
Giacinto
Magnolia
Mughetto

9 lettere
Clematide
Gelsomino

10 lettere
Fiordaliso

11 lettere
Caprifoglio

In cerca di fossili

Below this Word Fit puzzle there is a list of words.
Place the words correctly into the grid.

4 lettere
Ossa

5 lettere
Resti

6 lettere
Roccia
Strati

8 lettere
Ammonite
Impronta
Scoperta

9 lettere
Datazione
Organismo
Sedimenti

10 lettere
Estinzione
Evoluzione

12 lettere
Paleontologo

33   Quote by Jules Verne

Replace the numbers in the grid with the correct letters, and reveal the quote.

Hints: 25 = A   31 = D   8 = E   2 = N   1 = S

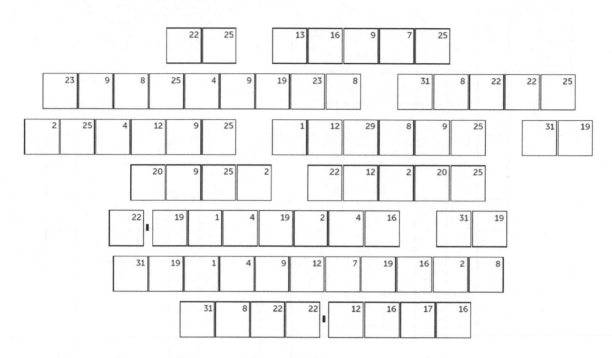

34   Quote by Galileo Galilei

Replace the numbers in the grid with the correct letters, and reveal the quote.

Hints: 8 = I   11 = L   12 = S   4 = U

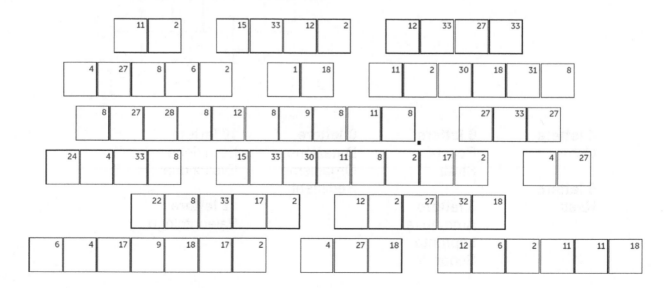

L'acqua in natura

The following words have been scrambled. Place the letters in the correct order.
For a less challenging version of this puzzle, please turn the page.

ACSATCA   _ _ _ _ _ _ _

IFMUE   _ _ _ _ _

GUANAL   _ _ _ _ _ _

AEMR   _ _ _ _

COEAON   _ _ _ _ _ _

LPUAED   _ _ _ _ _ _

GAIPOGI   _ _ _ _ _ _ _

OZOZP   _ _ _ _ _

OULLCESR   _ _ _ _ _ _ _ _

EEONGRST   _ _ _ _ _ _ _ _

AGNSTO   _ _ _ _ _ _

ENRTETOR   _ _ _ _ _ _ _ _

35b

L'acqua in natura

The words on the left have been scrambled. Place the letters in the correct order.

ACSATCA   C _ _ _ _ A

IFMUE   F _ _ _ _

GUANAL   L _ _ _ _ A

AEMR   M _ _ _

COEAON   O _ _ _ _ O

LPUAED   P _ _ _ _ E

GAIPOGI   P _ _ _ _ _ A

OZOZP   P _ _ _ _

OULLCESR   R _ _ C _ _ _ O

EEONGRST   S _ _ G _ _ _ E

AGNSTO   S _ _ _ _ O

ENRTETOR   T _ _ R _ _ _ E

I colori nella natura: Giallo

Translate the English words below the grid into Italian and find them in the Word Search. If this is too challenging, please turn the page for an easier puzzle.

```
Y  V  N  I  I  M  S  R  E  N  O  L  E  M  W
K  E  N  O  M  I  L  X  O  C  N  R  F  H  W
O  P  L  K  O  N  I  R  A  N  A  C  O  B  F
G  A  O  O  X  Y  O  S  I  C  R  A  N  S  E
H  N  E  W  S  T  S  I  A  M  E  T  I  I  O
H  E  L  O  S  A  R  B  M  A  F  A  C  N  B
K  S  G  W  R  C  R  O  C  J  F  T  L  G  F
J  A  U  A  S  O  M  I  M  X  A  A  U  A  U
Y  N  T  Y  G  L  R  V  G  N  Z  P  P  R  T
A  A  W  A  U  R  D  B  I  W  Y  O  W  Q  A
D  N  N  P  X  O  G  N  A  M  P  S  I  M  C
X  A  H  A  R  U  P  Y  I  H  H  K  Y  M  Q
T  T  V  P  N  T  H  E  J  J  B  Y  N  T  N
I  R  N  E  W  A  L  W  W  I  N  I  I  K  U
M  I  H  W  W  E  B  U  Y  Y  L  X  D  W  E
```

AMBER	MANGO	POTATO
PINEAPPLE	MELON	CHICK
BANANA	HONEY	MUSTARD
CANARY	MIMOSA	SUN
SUNFLOWER	DAFFODIL	DANDELION
LEMON	GOLD	EGG YOLK
SWEETCORN	PAPAYA	SAFFRON

I colori nella natura: Giallo

Find the Italian words below the grid in the Word Search puzzle. These are the same
Italian words as in 36a, but they're located in different positions on the grid.

```
O  J  R  Q  M  N  O  G  K  D  W  B  V  A  T
E  H  M  E  Y  X  Y  O  J  W  G  S  M  G  T
D  K  I  M  Z  D  J  V  J  M  O  B  M  L  V
H  Y  Z  X  M  K  V  X  E  T  R  G  Y  B  C
K  U  B  I  Y  P  A  L  A  A  N  A  N  A  B
V  J  E  T  H  V  O  N  A  R  E  F  F  A  Z
C  L  Z  U  K  N  N  C  Y  A  L  S  J  I  M
E  P  A  N  E  S  I  Y  A  S  O  M  I  M  N
N  A  T  T  C  Q  R  Z  P  S  S  P  M  A  L
O  K  V  S  A  N  A  N  A  A  A  O  R  O  H
M  S  B  I  Z  T  N  O  P  C  R  C  K  L  A
I  N  J  A  V  O  A  D  S  O  I  O  L  R  S
L  V  Z  M  C  A  C  P  T  S  G  F  P  O  S
D  K  B  Z  I  P  L  O  O  N  I  C  L  U  P
J  Y  Y  A  D  B  Z  G  Z  B  E  E  Z  T  M
```

AMBRA	MANGO	PATATA
ANANAS	MELONE	PULCINO
BANANA	MIELE	SENAPE
CANARINO	MIMOSA	SOLE
GIRASOLE	NARCISO	TARASSACO
LIMONE	ORO	TUORLO
MAIS	PAPAYA	ZAFFERANO

Il mappamondo 1

Translate the English words below the grid into Italian and find them in the Word Search. If this is too challenging, please turn the page for an easier puzzle.

```
O C U G K G A R Y Y C O I E P
J H F M O G A L E P I C R A R
F B M L R E T J T R R I L T X
E Y F R T S L I N A C T W S K
U O T R E S E D E U O N I O F
B W E A M A D D N P N A T C A
E R O T A U Q E I N F L J R E
M P L K I J C A T T E T E F Y
U N O T D O N I N R R A L L C
I J C Z N O H A O C E A A I X
F F R F P I T B C R N R T C O
E M I S F E R O O J Z T I N H
D N C F S I H Q L N A C P F A
E D I T R A L O S I B M A V T
S U G F Y K V A C E R O C S A
```

PLATEAU   CAPITAL   DESERT
ANTARCTICA   CIRCLE   DIAMETER
ARCHIPELAGO   CIRCUMFERENCE   EMISPHERE
AREA   CITY   EQUATOR
ARCTIC   BORDER   EAST
AXIS   CONTINENT   RIVER
ATLANTIC   COAST   GULF
BAY   DELTA   ISLAND

Il mappamondo 1

Find the Italian words below the grid in the Word Search puzzle. These are the same Italian words as in 37a, but they're located in different positions on the grid.

```
I  S  Q  X  A  T  O  V  H  S  C  O  G  I  L
E  X  X  R  O  G  A  L  E  P  I  C  R  A  T
O  L  O  C  R  I  C  Z  T  D  R  I  L  T  Z
T  S  E  N  E  N  I  F  N  O  C  T  Z  L  Y
R  D  O  S  F  I  E  D  E  C  O  N  E  E  E
E  W  Y  X  S  F  I  D  N  P  N  A  W  D  I
S  O  E  O  I  A  T  T  I  C  F  L  H  P  V
E  S  L  J  M  E  J  A  T  T  E  T  I  N  U
D  A  A  E  R  N  L  N  F  R  A  I  A  B
S  E  T  D  R  O  F  L  O  G  E  A  I  Z  X
U  R  I  I  A  T  S  O  C  F  N  F  T  B  U
O  A  P  T  T  A  S  U  I  M  Z  Q  J  N  R
K  T  A  R  I  U  D  U  O  V  A  I  Q  B  A
X  G  C  A  T  Q  M  P  F  M  D  R  J  K  N
V  X  A  C  Z  E  U  O  V  O  V  J  B  A  R
```

ALTOPIANO	CAPITALE	DESERTO
ANTARTIDE	CIRCOLO	DIAMETRO
ARCIPELAGO	CIRCONFERENZA	EMISFERO
AREA	CITTÀ	EQUATORE
ARTIDE	CONFINE	EST
ASSE	CONTINENTE	FIUME
ATLANTICO	COSTA	GOLFO
BAIA	DELTA	ISOLA

Il mappamondo 2

Translate the English words below the grid into Italian and find them in the Word Search. If this is too challenging, please turn the page for an easier puzzle.

```
O  B  M  Z  W  X  L  J  O  M  T  S  I  S  T
K  M  Q  V  A  B  X  Q  G  E  U  Z  T  I  A
J  H  L  D  I  N  O  W  A  D  M  R  P  K  H
V  O  N  Y  E  C  C  E  L  I  E  U  O  L  O
Q  B  B  A  E  N  I  D  U  T  I  G  N  O  L
H  O  P  A  N  M  F  R  T  E  S  E  A  I  E
K  V  N  N  I  A  I  O  S  R  Z  Q  I  R  L
Q  O  E  G  D  F  C  N  E  R  A  M  D  O  L
Y  H  L  A  U  P  A  J  V  A  R  I  I  T  A
B  I  L  T  T  Z  P  R  O  N  Z  U  R  N  R
A  I  A  N  I  C  R  C  G  E  I  O  E  O  A
L  C  V  O  T  X  T  O  L  O  P  V  M  M  P
A  O  N  M  A  R  U  N  A  I  P  S  Y  O  H
C  E  H  E  L  P  S  U  C  R  B  O  U  R  K
S  H  F  X  P  R  O  I  V  D  C  O  T  P  C
```

ISTHMUS	MOUNTAIN	POLE
LAKE	NATION	CAPE
LATITUDE	NORTH	SCALE
LONGITUDE	OCEAN	STRAIT
SEA	WEST	SOUTH
MEDITERRANEAN	PACIFIC	TOPOGRAPHY
MERIDIAN	PARALLEL	TROPICS
MILES	PLAIN	VALLEY

45

Il mappamondo 2

Find the Italian words below the grid in the Word Search puzzle. These are the same Italian words as in 38a, but they're located in different positions on the grid.

```
M  I  M  V  B  H  W  I  X  G  U  G  E  E  N
E  E  N  I  D  U  T  I  G  N  O  L  L  J  S
A  N  D  O  C  I  F  I  C  A  P  Q  L  C  C
I  I  A  I  F  A  R  G  O  P  O  T  A  P  N
U  D  R  R  T  G  T  L  U  D  N  L  V  O  X
H  U  U  O  L  E  L  L  A  R  A  P  V  G  J
O  T  N  T  I  A  R  E  N  O  I  Z  A  N  Y
D  I  A  N  G  R  J  R  G  N  D  I  I  G  X
T  T  I  O  M  T  S  I  A  S  I  C  L  U  O
U  A  P  M  N  M  C  A  T  N  R  I  G  L  A
V  L  U  O  A  O  M  R  N  N  E  P  I  V  O
F  B  Q  R  T  S  E  V  O  N  M  O  M  I  L
Q  L  E  P  U  T  O  W  M  P  E  R  L  G  G
I  G  V  D  T  L  V  T  G  M  G  T  J  O  T
C  X  M  O  N  A  E  C  O  A  R  X  A  N  P
```

ISTMO	MONTAGNA	POLO
LAGO	NAZIONE	PROMONTORIO
LATITUDINE	NORD	SCALA
LONGITUDINE	OCEANO	STRETTO
MARE	OVEST	SUD
MEDITERRANEO	PACIFICO	TOPOGRAFIA
MERIDIANO	PARALLELO	TROPICI
MIGLIA	PIANURA	VALLE

Alcune capitali

This freeform crossword has the clues in Italian. If you struggle to understand some of the clues, you can find them in English in the *Help Section* on page 130

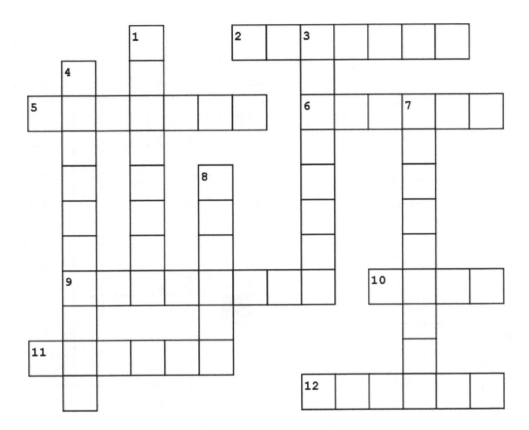

Orizzontali

2. Capitale della Cina
5. Capitale del Kenya
6. Capitale delle Bahamas
9. Capitale dell'Indonesia
10. Capitale dell'Italia
11. Capitale del Regno Unito
12. Capitale dell'Albania

Verticali

1. Capitale della Polonia
3. Capitale dell'Australia
4. Capitale degli Stati Uniti
7. Capitale della Svezia
8. Capitale del Canada

Il pianeta Terra

This freeform crossword has the clues in Italian. If you struggle to understand some of the clues, you can find them in English in the *Help Section* on page 130

Orizzontali

2. Linea verticale immaginaria tra Polo Nord e Polo Sud

4. Lo strato più esterno della terra

9. Altezza sopra il livello del mare

10. Moto della terra intorno al sole

12. L'insieme dei gas che avvolge la terra

Verticali

1. La terra ne fa una al giorno

3. La foresta pluviale più grande

5. Divide la terra in due emisferi (nord e sud)

6. Piccola isola a forma di ciambella

7. L'aria che respiriamo

8. Il colore della terra visto dallo Spazio

11. La forza che fa cadere le cose

Stagioni: estate

Match the Italian words on the left, to the English words on the right.

caldo	crab
sole	shell
luce	mosquito
girasole	cricket
zanzara	June
conchiglia	apricot
granchio	peach
grillo	heat
spiaggia	light
giugno	sunflower
albicocca	beach
pesca	sun

Piante medicinali

Match the Italian words on the left, to the English words on the right.

calendula	linseed
ortica	ginger
iperico	valerian
zenzero	chilli
camomilla	marigold
valeriana	lavender
peperoncino	hypericum
curcuma	eucalyptus
lavanda	horsetail
equiseto	chamomile
semi di lino	nettle
eucalipto	turmeric

Civiltà antiche

Below this Word Fit puzzle there is a list of words.
Place the words correctly into the grid.

5 lettere
Greci
Egizi

6 lettere
Assiri
Fenici
Ittiti
Romani
Sumeri

7 lettere
Cretesi
Micenei

8 lettere
Etruschi

10 lettere
Babilonesi

11 lettere
Cartaginesi

La forza dei venti

Below this Word Fit puzzle there is a list of words.
Place the words correctly into the grid.

6 lettere
Brezza
Bufera
Tifone

7 lettere
Ciclone
Tornado
Turbine
Uragano
Arietta

8 lettere
Burrasca
Corrente
Tempesta
Tormenta

10 lettere
Venticello

45   Quote by Johann Wolfgang von Goethe

Replace the numbers in the grid with the correct letters, and reveal the quote.

Hints: 24 = C   32 = D   20 = I   26 = O   8 = R

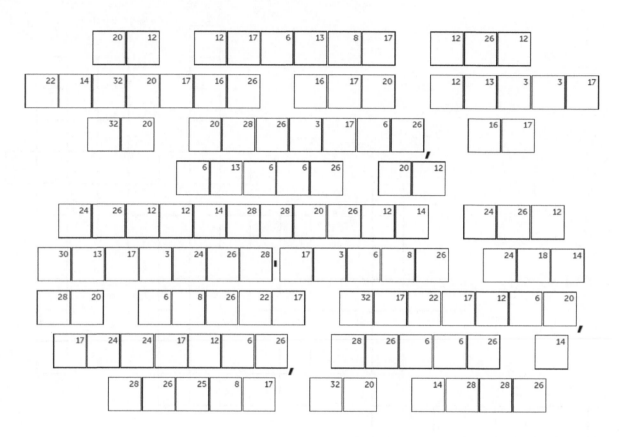

46   Quote by Immanuel Kant

Replace the numbers in the grid with the correct letters, and reveal the quote.

Hints: 24 = G   30 = I   6 = N   22 = O

Cose della giungla

The following words have been scrambled. Place the letters in the correct order.
For a less challenging version of this puzzle, please turn the page.

IEFLC _ _ _ _ _

ELRAIB _ _ _ _ _ _

AMISMCI _ _ _ _ _ _ _

LPPPOAAGAL _ _ _ _ _ _ _ _ _

ILLROAG _ _ _ _ _ _ _

AAGOIUGR _ _ _ _ _ _ _ _

OMRIFHEERIC _ _ _ _ _ _ _ _ _ _ _

IPARTO _ _ _ _ _ _

DNAOCAAN _ _ _ _ _ _ _ _

NACTOU _ _ _ _ _ _

IAOPIGG _ _ _ _ _ _ _

UISFC _ _ _ _ _

Cose della giungla

The words on the left have been scrambled. Place the letters in the correct order.

IEFLC   F _ _ _ _

ELRAIB   A _ _ _ _ I

AMISMCI   S _ _ _ _ _ A

LPPPOAAGAL   P _ _ _ A _ _ _ _ O

ILLROAG   G _ _ _ _ _ A

AAGOIUGR   G _ _ _ _ _ _ O

OMRIFHEERIC   F _ _ M _ _ H _ _ _ E

IPARTO   T _ _ _ _ O

DNAOCAAN   A _ _ C _ _ _ _ A

NACTOU   T _ _ _ _ O

IAOPIGG   P _ _ _ _ _ A

UISFC   F _ _ _ _

Aggettivi del mare/oceano

Translate the English words below the grid into Italian and find them in the Word Search. If this is too challenging, please turn the page for an easier puzzle.

```
S  O  O  T  T  A  I  P  M  O  S  S  O  A  W
I  P  K  Q  G  O  R  R  U  Z  Z  A  F  F  O
M  F  U  A  C  O  T  A  N  I  F  N  O  C  S
P  M  O  M  F  E  O  D  I  B  R  O  T  V  O
E  L  S  O  E  T  N  E  R  A  P  S  A  R  T
T  J  N  S  O  G  R  G  T  W  H  S  P  M  S
U  D  E  O  T  O  G  V  I  X  T  O  S  Y  E
O  O  M  L  A  C  P  I  Y  O  C  D  E  O  P
S  T  M  O  N  I  L  L  A  T  S  I  R  C  M
O  A  I  C  I  N  L  J  O  N  O  D  C  I  E
O  L  L  I  U  Q  N  A  R  T  T  N  N  F  T
N  A  L  R  Q  F  Z  Z  A  A  E  E  I  I  P
H  S  S  E  N  T  N  S  I  R  I  L  T  C  M
R  S  I  P  I  A  I  R  H  H  U  P  I  A  A
A  G  I  T  A  T  O  F  C  N  Q  S  M  P  R
```

ROUGH	POLLUTED	BOUNDLESS
BLUE	CHOPPY	SPLENDID
CALM	PEACEFUL	FOAMY
CLEAR	DANGEROUS	STORMY
CRYSTAL-CLEAR	EVEN	MURKY
HUGE	DEEP	TRANQUIL
FIERCE (STRONG)	QUIET	TRANSPARENT
RIPPLY	SALTY	VAST

Aggettivi del mare/oceano

Find the Italian words below the grid in the Word Search puzzle. These are the same Italian words as in 48a, but they're located in different positions on the grid.

```
S  X  M  A  P  O  T  A  N  I  U  Q  N  I  F
T  P  Q  U  I  E  T  O  M  O  I  J  N  F  M
E  I  U  R  B  Z  Y  P  G  M  V  N  O  O  L
M  O  L  M  Y  J  E  F  M  L  W  L  T  O  O
P  D  O  O  E  T  N  E  R  A  P  S  A  R  T
E  I  J  S  U  G  N  B  P  C  Q  Z  P  A  A
S  B  X  O  W  S  G  A  S  J  U  O  S  I  N
T  R  S  L  O  H  C  I  P  F  U  D  E  H  I
O  O  X  O  N  I  L  L  A  T  S  I  R  C  F
S  T  I  C  F  L  N  M  U  N  F  D  C  S  N
O  L  L  I  U  Q  N  A  R  T  T  N  N  A  O
T  M  C  R  A  Z  Z  U  R  R  O  E  I  L  C
S  O  M  E  A  G  I  T  A  T  O  L  B  A  S
A  T  U  P  O  D  N  O  F  O  R  P  S  T  H
V  T  O  O  H  P  I  A  T  T  O  S  S  O  M
```

AGITATO	INQUINATO	SCONFINATO
AZZURRO	MOSSO	SPLENDIDO
CALMO	PACIFICO	SPUMEGGIANTE
CHIARO	PERICOLOSO	TEMPESTOSO
CRISTALLINO	PIATTO	TORBIDO
IMMENSO	PROFONDO	TRANQUILLO
IMPETUOSO	QUIETO	TRASPARENTE
INCRESPATO	SALATO	VASTO

I colori nella natura: Verde

Translate the English words below the grid into Italian and find them in the Word Search. If this is too challenging, please turn the page for an easier puzzle.

```
E A S I C A N I P S R S I L Y
Z U I L O C C O R B U I I Y Y
N K W L F C X L T D E B K Q V
P O I E O S I O D L A R E M S
Q O K S I N I L O I G A F B O
T I I I C O L O I R T E C V U
N H G P R O A M Y S S G R I P
E C A V A L L E T T A O X Z O
B C R R C O O Z S B S B T O G
A O A J E V C Z V M A I Z N Z
H N P A X A U E A G U T T A L
A I S S X C R R F I T G N D P
M F A E K B I P P R R D E E Y
H C W O A N I H C C U Z C S M
O U M P O D A C O V A D A I G
```

ASPARAGUS	GRASS	PARSLEY
AVOCADO	GREEN BEANS	FROG
BASIL	FENNEL	ROSEMARY
BROCCOLI	JADE	ARUGULA
ARTICHOKE	KIWI	CELERY
GRASSHOPPER	LETTUCE	EMERALD
CABBAGE	MINT	SPINACH
CUCUMBER	PEAS	COURGETTE

57

I colori nella natura: Verde

Find the Italian words below the grid in the Word Search puzzle. These are the same
Italian words as in 49a, but they're located in different positions on the grid.

```
U L Z U X X O I G A R A P S A
A I C A N I P S T A G D M D N
D W R Y C N A T N E M X P S I
J I M G Y I E A F O R M M N H
W K O O O L O M E Z Z E R P C
T X L D L O I N H V R V O P C
A H O A O I H T I A L T N C U
L E V C I G C F L R E R A K Z
O A A O R A C D O W A R D E H
C G C V T F O G C Q C M E U S
U U C A E F N O C I L I S A B
R T N R C L I W O W F L C O L
J T B S H I F F R W R H N J R
F A D A I G O Q B E L E I P N
I L L E S I P J J K F W C B V
```

ASPARAGI   ERBA   PREZZEMOLO
AVOCADO   FAGIOLINI   RANA
BASILICO   FINOCCHIO   ROSMARINO
BROCCOLI   GIADA   RUCOLA
CARCIOFO   KIWI   SEDANO
CAVALLETTA   LATTUGA   SMERALDO
CAVOLO   MENTA   SPINACI
CETRIOLO   PISELLI   ZUCCHINA

Translate the English words below the grid into Italian and find them in the Word Search. If this is too challenging, please turn the page for an easier puzzle.

```
D F T F B N A P H C O T F S P
Q X N O E P P H H A S H S E R
S O V D O G O D A V A C H D E
M X M M N E N O I S O R E I I
B V I O T I N A R G X K L M S
A C F E S C Z O L Y O A I E T
E V R S O I U I I B L M S N O
R R A Y R F E O Q Z L G S T R
A O E L A R E N I M A A O A I
C N Z Q A E D A C M T M F Z A
L E M N N P S T X J S S R I Z
A R U T T U R T S A I C C O R
C R H H I S E O T A R T S N F
J E R E N E C R M A C O P E T
A T S O R C G G E C O B T O D
```

LIMESTONE	FOSSIL	ROCK
QUARRY	GRANITE	CLIFF
ASH	CAVE	SEDIMENTATION
CRYSTAL	LAVA	LAYER
CRUST	MAGMA	STRUCTURE
EPOCH	MINERAL	SURFACE
EROSION	PUMICE	EARTH
FORMATION	PREHISTORY	SOIL

Geologia

Find the Italian words below the grid in the Word Search puzzle. These are the same Italian words as in 50a, but they're located in different positions on the grid.

```
S  K  E  S  J  U  J  U  P  P  N  Z  L  A  S
Z  E  I  C  I  F  R  E  P  U  S  M  A  X  T
L  N  D  A  R  E  I  L  G  O  C  S  C  E  R
Y  O  T  I  N  A  R  G  A  I  C  C  O  R  A
E  I  Z  R  M  P  O  M  I  C  E  X  P  A  T
K  Z  A  O  E  E  N  O  I  S  O  R  E  C  O
B  A  W  T  L  L  N  K  S  D  A  V  A  L  L
Y  M  H  S  A  R  U  T  T  U  R  T  S  A  J
F  R  Z  I  R  O  L  L  A  T  S  I  R  C  H
K  O  W  E  E  N  C  F  T  Z  Y  U  J  R  P
A  F  O  R  N  E  Y  E  E  L  I  S  S  O  F
V  J  X  P  I  R  R  K  A  T  S  O  R  C  M
A  M  G  A  M  R  I  O  J  Q  A  D  N  Q  N
C  I  Z  C  A  E  R  E  N  E  C  M  E  E  O
R  B  V  Z  A  T  T  O  R  G  E  M  O  W  Z
```

CALCARE	FOSSILE	ROCCIA
CAVA	GRANITO	SCOGLIERA
CENERE	GROTTA	SEDIMENTAZIONE
CRISTALLO	LAVA	STRATO
CROSTA	MAGMA	STRUTTURA
EPOCA	MINERALE	SUPERFICIE
EROSIONE	POMICE	TERRA
FORMAZIONE	PREISTORIA	TERRENO

Geografia dell'Italia

This freeform crossword has the clues in Italian. If you struggle to understand some of the clues, you can find them in English in the *Help Section* on page 130

Orizzontali

3. Isola del Mar di Sicilia
6. La città del gianduiotto
7. Isola a sud della Corsica
8. Viene anche chiamata La Serenissima
9. Il tacco dello stivale italiano
10. La città di Giulietta e Romeo

Verticali

1. Gruppo montuoso delle Alpi
2. Un grande lago d'Italia
4. La patria di San Francesco
5. Il mare dell'Abruzzo
9. La più grande pianura italiana
11. Vulcano sopra Catania

Che tempo fa?

This freeform crossword has the clues in Italian. If you struggle to understand some of the clues, you can find them in English in the *Help Section* on page 131

Orizzontali

2. Si scioglie quando piove
7. La scienza dei fenomeni atmosferici
9. Venti tropicali che portano pioggia
10. La quantità di vapore acqueo nell'aria
11. Scala della temperature
12. Vento caldo proveniente dall'Africa

Verticali

1. Misura la pressione dell'aria
3. Misura la temperatura
4. Scarica elettrica durante il temporale
5. Le goccioline sull'erba, al mattino
6. Pioggia di palline di ghiaccio
8. Le aspettative di che tempo farà

Animali e versi

Match the Italian words on the left, to the Italian words on the right.

leone	ulula
lupo	gloglotta
cinghiale	tuba
asino	ruggisce
elefante	gracida
rana	barrisce
scoiattolo	sibila
anatra	raglia
tacchino	squittisce
serpente	grugnisce
piccione	bramisce
cervo	starnazza

Paesi e lingue ufficiali

Match the Italian words on the left, to the Italian words on the right.

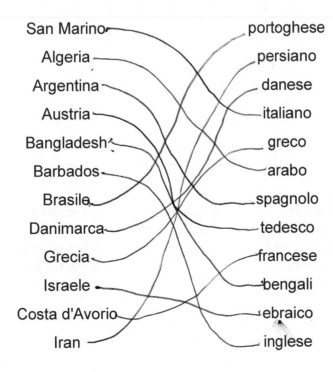

San Marino	portoghese
Algeria	persiano
Argentina	danese
Austria	italiano
Bangladesh	greco
Barbados	arabo
Brasile	spagnolo
Danimarca	tedesco
Grecia	francese
Israele	bengali
Costa d'Avorio	ebraico
Iran	inglese

La cellula animale

Below this Word Fit puzzle there is a list of words.
Place the words correctly into the grid.

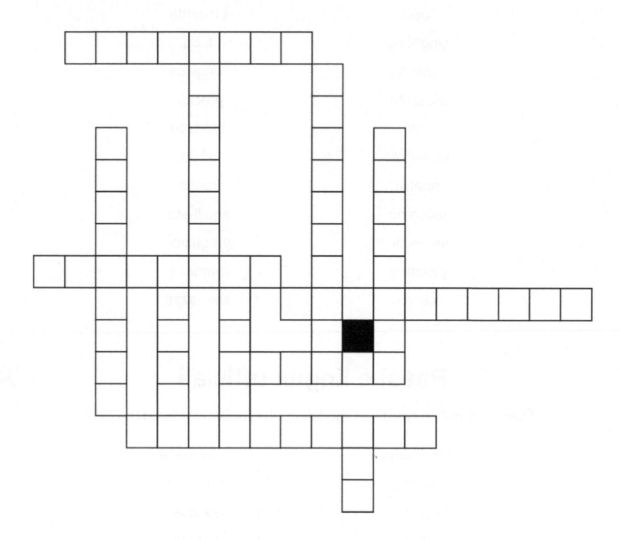

3 lettere
DNA

6 lettere
Enzimi
Lipidi
Nucleo

8 lettere
Lisosomi
Membrana
Proteine
Ribosomi

9 lettere
Cromosomi

10 lettere
Aminoacidi
Citoplasma
Mitocondri

I grandi esploratori

Below this Word Fit puzzle there is a list of words.
Place the words correctly into the grid.

4 lettere
Cook
Polo

5 lettere
Drake

6 lettere
Caboto
Elcano

7 lettere
Colombo

8 lettere
Amundsen
Vespucci

9 lettere
Armstrong
Magellano
Malaspina

10 lettere
Shackleton

11 lettere
Livingstone

57 Chinese proverb

Replace the numbers in the grid with the correct letters, and reveal the quote.

Hints: 30 = A   4 = L   21 = M   20 = 0   3 = S

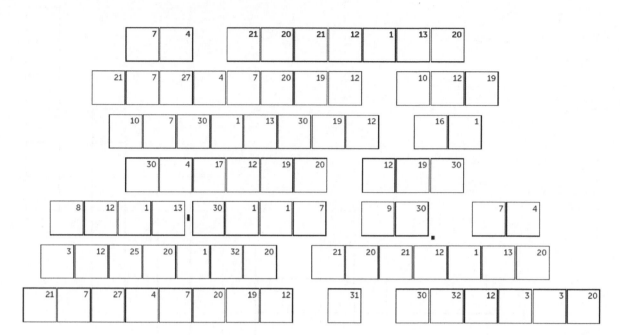

58 Quote by Michel de Montaigne

Replace the numbers in the grid with the correct letters, and reveal the quote.

Hints: 6 = A   16 = E   29 = L   31 = N   21 = R

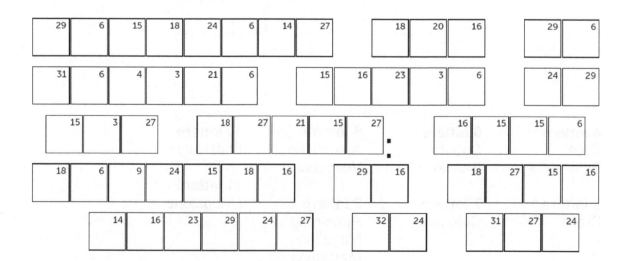

Andiamo a caccia

The following words have been scrambled. Place the letters in the correct order.
For a less challenging version of this puzzle, please turn the page.

RDPEA   _ _ _ _ _

GGNASVAELI   _ _ _ _ _ _ _ _ _

ULEICF   _ _ _ _ _ _

RTITOPLEIE   _ _ _ _ _ _ _ _ _

ARCAUTCIC   _ _ _ _ _ _ _ _

RCAEFIC   _ _ _ _ _ _ _

CAOR   _ _ _ _

PARALOTP   _ _ _ _ _ _ _ _

RMPNIAOT   _ _ _ _ _ _ _

OOCSB   _ _ _ _ _

PRASO   _ _ _ _ _

NILOCOBO   _ _ _ _ _ _ _ _

Andiamo a caccia

The words on the left have been scrambled. Place the letters in the correct order.

RDPEA   P _ _ _ _

GGNASVAELI   S _ _ _ _ G _ _ _ A

ULEICF   F _ _ _ _ E

RTITOPLEIE   P _ _ I _ _ T _ _ E

ARCAUTCIC   C _ _ _ U _ _ _ A

RCAEFIC   F _ _ _ _ _ A

CAOR   A _ _ _

PARALOTP   T _ _ _ P _ _ A

RMPNIAOT   I _ _ R _ _ _ A

OOCSB   B _ _ _ _

PRASO   S _ _ _ _

NILOCOBO   B _ _ _ C _ _ O

Translate the English words below the grid into Italian and find them in the Word Search. If this is too challenging, please turn the page for an easier puzzle.

```
K L H X C T H O W C T B J Y Q
R C W E G J T W W E C U O D K
L Y N P N O L L A R O C O C B
A L R E P A K N U M R V D T D
R O L A P I S L A Z Z U L I W
J N Z N L O B E T N A M A I D
M I D I U R Q E S E H C R U T
O B S R V I E C I N O O E P D
L U V A H F E P T O G E M D K
L R D M G F M W E C W I S O R
I S J A T A G A M R K E A U R
R B D U A Z M L A I D L X D E
E C Y Q I B E W O Z R A U Q A
B X R C R N M W P F P P M H O
K Q X A N A I D I S S O E A N
```

AQUAMARINE	JADE	QUARTZ
AGATE	LAPIS LAZULI	RUBY
AMBER	MOTHER-OF-PEARL	EMERALD
AMETHYST	ONYX	TOPAZ
BERYL	OPAL	TURQUOISE
CORAL	OBSIDIAN	SAPPHIRE
DIAMOND	PEARL	ZIRCON

Pietre preziose e gemme

Find the Italian words below the grid in the Word Search puzzle. These are the same Italian words as in 60a, but they're located in different positions on the grid.

```
L Y X F M O I D N J S U B S R
H A N I R A M A U Q C A O G D
S L P E P E L P H T W N I B G
T R K I N F O R I F F A Z I F
S E H E S E H C R U T I A G F
W P Q O D L A R E M S D P J Y
W E T N A M A I D N A I O E S
P R I I T M T Z K P O S T Y L
N D K B A G S I Z P O S M H X
T A S U G H I K A U L O D W M
P M J R A L T L O L L I R E B
L C K M R J E F T R A I H X R
K K Q E B M M C O Z R A U Q S
V L Y U M X A Y E N O C R I Z
X Q R M A L R E P E C I N O J
```

ACQUAMARINA	GIADA	QUARZO
AGATA	LAPISLAZZULI	RUBINO
AMBRA	MADREPERLA	SMERALDO
AMETISTA	ONICE	TOPAZIO
BERILLO	OPALE	TURCHESE
CORALLO	OSSIDIANA	ZAFFIRO
DIAMANTE	PERLA	ZIRCONE

Il mondo dei rettili e degli anfibi

Translate the English words below the grid into Italian and find them in the Word Search. If this is too challenging, please turn the page for an easier puzzle.

```
A  I  C  S  I  B  M  S  O  P  S  O  R  W  X
E  T  N  O  E  L  A  M  A  C  I  W  L  Y  L
T  A  N  C  C  O  R  J  O  F  O  T  Q  W  D
N  R  E  S  W  C  B  E  B  Y  W  E  O  E  I
E  B  M  I  A  L  O  T  R  E  C  U  L  N  F
P  E  F  L  V  D  C  D  A  R  E  P  I  V  E
R  T  Z  I  P  A  G  U  R  A  T  R  A  T  W
E  R  J  S  C  R  D  Q  D  I  A  Y  D  A  O
S  E  M  A  U  Q  S  Y  N  N  L  U  Y  M  F
O  V  F  B  E  R  O  T  A  G  I  L  L  A  Z
T  D  S  H  H  T  I  C  M  N  O  K  O  N  R
G  D  H  N  Z  N  O  N  A  M  I  A  C  A  V
M  Z  S  N  F  N  T  E  L  J  X  K  E  U  G
V  H  R  Z  D  V  J  V  A  X  P  B  G  G  I
I  Q  C  A  N  L  T  L  S  R  G  Z  Z  I  K
```

ALLIGATOR	COBRA	TOAD
ANACONDA	CROCODILE	SALAMANDER
BASILISK	GECKO	SNAKE
GRASS SNAKE	IGUANA	SCALES
BOA	LIZARD	TURTLE
CAYMAN	PYTHON	VERTEBRATES
CHAMELEON	FROG	VIPER

Il mondo dei rettili e degli anfibi

Find the Italian words below the grid in the Word Search puzzle. These are the same Italian words as in 61a, but they're located in different positions on the grid.

```
A V W A R B O C N G W Y L W G
P F E N O T I P C L E E N W N
Y T M A P S C G U F T X A G L
V Q A U S F A C D T N A K A N
N N U G O C E G A Z O D B Q N
L Y Q I R R W R I L E N N Y X
E G S A T Q T I L I L O B O T
P E R O T A G I L L A C Y N M
A K L C R A R D N A M A L A S
V A R U F D L B V B A N Q M V
Z N G I O N X D E F C A Q I I
I A I C S I B P N T H O P A R
K R C F J E T N E P R E S C V
B O C S I L I S A B R E Z T X
C P N B F K Q G Q A W S V X G
```

ALLIGATORE	COBRA	ROSPO
ANACONDA	COCCODRILLO	SALAMANDRA
BASILISCO	GECO	SERPENTE
BISCIA	IGUANA	SQUAME
BOA	LUCERTOLA	TARTARUGA
CAIMANO	PITONE	VERTEBRATI
CAMALEONTE	RANA	VIPERA

I colori nella natura: Bianco

62a

Translate the English words below the grid into Italian and find them in the Word Search. If this is too challenging, please turn the page for an easier puzzle.

```
Q Q U P K R X M N A N O T E C
B G O Q P D A P B P C C Y A Y
C S F P E V E N E A G U L E B
J Y E N W C J V V L W L R G M
B C T Y O X C O E R A C L A C
S I T R N Q L I N E B P R L J
A N A T G F U R A P M M J O B
W I L N I C H O C O O F C V N
R L V O C N S V U L L H C U P
E L R I D O O A B X O H J N A
L E R L S S S X I Y C N P Y I
X N V G S I O P N V O U Q U D
O N G A L R F R I L O Z F W V
M A Z A L K P Q X N D A C X E
U C P T P U Q J H N O G L E G
```

GARLIC
IVORY
HAWTHORN
SNOWDROP
BELUGA
LIMESTONE
CALLA

WHITE KIDNEY BEANS
CAULIFLOWER
SWAN
DOVE
TEETH
MILK
MARBLE

SNOW
CLOUD
GOOSE
BONES
SHEEP
PEARL
RICE

73

I colori nella natura: Bianco

Find the Italian words below the grid in the Word Search puzzle. These are the same Italian words as in 62a, but they're located in different positions on the grid.

```
B  L  T  N  M  T  C  B  A  G  U  L  E  B  F
S  Y  C  Y  J  I  N  I  L  L  E  N  N  A  C
N  J  D  K  G  K  I  A  O  O  R  H  G  B  G
F  H  C  N  X  J  T  N  V  S  O  L  Y  M  A
E  D  O  R  L  T  N  C  U  J  I  D  H  O  L
Z  R  N  Y  E  W  E  O  N  O  F  R  A  L  U
T  S  V  O  E  H  D  S  G  S  L  V  R  O  F
G  U  W  R  R  V  W  P  A  T  O  J  O  C  V
D  N  T  B  A  P  E  I  H  R  V  C  C  R  O
G  F  Y  D  C  R  V  N  I  S  A  W  E  P  K
L  M  P  G  L  I  E  O  A  C  C  S  P  I  Z
X  W  O  A  A  S  N  M  L  C  H  G  R  Q  W
K  K  D  S  C  T  D  R  L  L  U  E  Z  A  A
T  B  N  S  Y  G  G  A  A  K  O  B  E  C  M
A  V  L  O  C  S  K  M  C  C  W  Z  Z  H  N
```

AGLIO	CANNELLINI	NEVE
AVORIO	CAVOLFIORE	NUVOLA
BIANCOSPINO	CIGNO	OCA
BUCANEVE	COLOMBA	OSSA
BELUGA	DENTI	PECORA
CALCARE	LATTE	PERLA
CALLA	MARMO	RISO

This freeform crossword has the clues in Italian. If you struggle to understand some of the clues, you can find them in English in the *Help Section* on page 131

Orizzontali

3. Paese dove si trova il Taj Mahal

5. Tombe reali dell'Egitto

7. Il Paese che ospita il muro più lungo del mondo

8. Lo stato del Golden Gate Bridge

10. Una capitale europea conosciuta per il Big Ben

11. Città toscana con la torre pendente

12. Complesso megalitico del Wiltshire

Verticali

1. Civiltà che costruì Machu Picchu

2. Famose cascate tra Canada e Stati Uniti

4. La torre più famosa a Parigi

6. Cittadella che domina Atene

9. Il più grande anfiteatro del mondo

L'inquinamento

This freeform crossword has the clues in Italian. If you struggle to understand some of the clues, you can find them in English in the *Help Section* on page 131

Orizzontale

4. Veicoli che vanno e vengono

6. Materiali di scarto

8. Quando una specie cessa di esistere

10. Protegge la terra dai raggi ultravioletti

11. Sinonimo di velenoso e nocivo

12. Pericolosissime quelle di Chernobyl

Verticale

1. Materiale di molte bottiglie d'acqua

2. Usati in agricoltura contro i parassiti

3. Il riscaldamento globale li fa sciogliere

5. Persona che lotta per l'ambiente

7. Gas inodore e infiammabile

9. Inquina l'aria delle metropoli

Andiamo a pescare

The following words have been scrambled. Place the letters in the correct order.
For a less challenging version of this puzzle, please turn the page.

TREE   _ _ _ _

AABRC   _ _ _ _ _

OAM   _ _ _

CSEA   _ _ _ _

ZLAEN   _ _ _ _ _

NANAC   _ _ _ _ _

ELLUMNIOL   _ _ _ _ _ _ _ _ _

AVILTIS   _ _ _ _ _ _ _

IDSAE   _ _ _ _ _

CSOECHI   _ _ _ _ _ _ _

BAAL   _ _ _ _

AEEIAGTGGNLL   _ _ _ _ _ _ _ _ _ ___

Andiamo a pescare

The words on the left have been scrambled. Place the letters in the correct order.

TREE	R E T E
AABRC	B A R C A
OAM	A M O
CSEA	E S C A
ZLAEN	L E N Z A
NANAC	C A N N A
ELLUMNIOL	M U L I N E L L O
AVILTIS	S T I V A L I
IDSAE	S E D I A
CSOECHI	S E C C H I O
BAAL	A L B A
AEEIAGTGGNLL	G A L L E G G I A N T E

Stagioni: autunno

Match the Italian words on the left, to the English words on the right.

raccolto	migration
pioggia	hazelnut
foglia	mushroom
zucca	fog
nebbia	acorn
ghianda	spider
castagna	October
ragno	chestnut
fungo	rain
migrazione	harvest
ottobre	leaf
nocciola	pumpkin

Visitiamo le grotte

Match the Italian words on the left, to the English words on the right.

speleologo	cavern
calcare	stalagmite
stalattite	well
stalagmite	tunnel
caverna	excavation
pozzo	recess
sotterraneo	speleologist
erosione	vault
galleria	erosion
volta	limestone
nicchia	underground
scavo	stalactite

Valute del mondo

Below this Word Fit puzzle there is a list of words.
Place the words correctly into the grid.

3 lettere	**5 lettere**	**6 lettere**	**7 lettere**
Yen	Riyal	Corona	Dollaro
	Rublo	Dinaro	Fiorino
4 lettere	Rupia	Franco	
Euro		Libbra	**8 lettere**
Lira			Scellino
Peso			Sterlina
Rand			
Yuan			

La teoria dell'evoluzione

Below this Word Fit puzzle there is a list of words.
Place the words correctly into the grid.

6 lettere
Specie

7 lettere
Origini

8 lettere
Antenati
Genetica

9 lettere
Caratteri
Mutazioni
Selezione

10 lettere
Estinzione

11 lettere
Adattamento
Discendenti
Generazioni

13 lettere
Sopravvivenza

Quote by Vincent van Gogh

Replace the numbers in the grid with the correct letters, and reveal the quote.

Hints: 8 = C   25 = E   32 = I   28 = P   1 = T

```
[32]   [28][25][24][8][11][1][18][6][32]   [24][11][5][5][18]

   [8][31][25]   [32][14]   [33][11][6][25]   [3]

[28][25][6][32][8][18][14][18][24][18]   [25]   [14][11]

            [1][25][33][28][25][24][1][11]

[1][25][6][6][32][29][32][14][25] ,   [33][11]   [5][18][5]

   [31][11][5][5][18]   [33][11][32]

[8][18][5][24][32][20][25][6][11][1][18]   [26][19][25][32]

   [28][25][6][32][8][18][14][32]   [19][5][11]

         [6][11][16][32][18][5][25]

[24][19][13][13][32][8][32][25][5][1][25]   [28][25][6]

[6][32][33][11][5][25][6][25]   [11]   [1][25][6][6][11]
```

Quote by John Webster

Replace the numbers in the grid with the correct letters, and reveal the quote.

Hints: 2 = A   1 = C   17 = I   23 = P   12 = T

```
[23][27][11][18][17][2][31][3]   [1][26][27]   [15][28][17]

[13][1][1][27][28][28][17]   [17][11]   [15][2][16][16][17][2]

   [1][2][11][12][17][11][3] ,   [31][27][11][12][30][27]

[17][11]   [30][27][2][28][12][7]   [23][17][2][11][15][3][11][3]
```

Stati dell'America meridionale

The following words have been scrambled. Place the letters in the correct order.
For a less challenging version of this puzzle, please turn the page.

TGNNIREAA   _ _ _ _ _ _ _ _ _

IAOVLIB   _ _ _ _ _ _ _

LSBRAEI   _ _ _ _ _ _ _

EICL   _ _ _ _

OICABLMO   _ _ _ _ _ _ _ _

UCDRAOE   _ _ _ _ _ _ _

NYGAUA   _ _ _ _ _ _

AAYRUAPG   _ _ _ _ _ _ _ _

ÙRPE   _ _ _ _

MUNSREAI   _ _ _ _ _ _ _ _

GUUYUAR   _ _ _ _ _ _ _

UVAENZLEE   _ _ _ _ _ _ _ _ _

Stati dell'America meridionale

The words on the left have been scrambled. Place the letters in the correct order.

TGNNIREAA	A _ _ _ N _ _ _ A
IAOVLIB	B _ _ _ _ _ A
LSBRAEI	B _ _ _ _ E
EICL	C _ _ _
OICABLMO	C _ _ _ _ _ A
UCDRAOE	E _ _ _ _ R
NYGAUA	G _ _ _ A
AAYRUAPG	P _ _ _ G _ _ Y
ÙRPE	P _ _ _
MUNSREAI	S _ _ I _ _ _ E
GUUYUAR	U _ _ _ _ _ Y
UVAENZLEE	V _ _ _ Z _ _ _ A

Cambiamento climatico

Translate the English words below the grid into Italian and find them in the Word Search. If this is too challenging, please turn the page for an easier puzzle.

```
A  J  F  N  Z  K  T  Z  H  Q  Q  X  A  N  O  R  O  B
E  I  T  T  A  L  A  M  N  I  D  N  E  C  N  I  I  B
H  O  Q  X  A  R  U  T  A  R  E  P  M  E  T  S  L  L
C  I  N  O  I  S  S  I  M  E  S  V  N  L  H  C  O  B
I  N  O  I  V  U  L  L  A  N  E  S  P  C  D  N  R  Y
R  O  T  N  E  M  A  T  T  U  R  F  S  L  Q  S  T  Y
B  I  K  K  E  N  O  I  Z  A  T  S  E  R  O  F  E  D
B  Z  C  I  N  O  I  Z  A  T  I  P  I  C  E  R  P  S
A  A  I  R  T  S  A  S  I  D  F  S  I  C  C  I  T  A
F  L  T  A  Z  P  I  L  I  B  I  T  S  U  B  M  O  C
O  A  R  I  E  Y  O  A  T  I  C  I  R  T  T  E  L  E
R  S  O  T  N  E  M  A  D  L  A  C  S  I  R  R  U  S
W  E  P  S  O  I  T  N  A  Z  Z  I  L  I  T  R  E  F
H  T  S  E  I  M  D  E  H  C  I  R  A  C  S  I  D  R
T  R  A  R  S  L  Y  L  W  F  O  D  X  H  X  K  B  S
P  X  R  A  O  T  N  E  M  A  N  I  U  Q  N  I  I  Q
G  N  T  C  R  P  T  W  Y  W  E  N  O  B  R  A  C  J
O  K  Q  L  E  V  Q  Z  V  F  U  F  U  M  O  E  Y  U
```

FLOODS	EMISSIONS	DISEASES
FUELS	EROSION	OIL
COAL	FUMES	PRECIPITATIONS
FAMINE	ELECTRICITY	DROUGHT
DEFORESTATION	FERTILIZERS	OVERHEATING
DESERTIFICATION	FIRES	EXPLOITATION
DISASTERS	FACTORIES	TEMPERATURE
LANDFILLS	POLLUTION	TRANSPORTATION

Cambiamento climatico

Find the Italian words below the grid in the Word Search puzzle. These are the same Italian words as in 73a, but they're located in different positions on the grid.

```
D  I  N  O  I  Z  A  T  I  P  I  C  E  R  P  W  E  Z
X  E  O  T  N  E  M  A  T  T  U  R  F  S  O  L  K  O
T  N  S  N  W  P  Z  E  N  O  I  S  O  R  E  Q  H  X
A  O  I  E  A  D  I  Z  A  X  E  I  T  T  A  L  A  M
A  I  P  M  R  O  N  G  Z  J  P  F  T  U  Y  E  V  E
W  Z  Z  A  U  T  O  O  Z  Z  Q  R  X  Y  X  X  A  H
C  A  D  D  T  N  I  L  I  B  I  T  S  U  B  M  O  C
Z  T  Q  L  A  E  Z  F  L  C  C  A  R  B  O  N  E  I
Y  S  U  A  R  M  A  A  I  N  O  I  V  U  L  L  A  R
D  E  R  C  E  A  L  T  T  C  D  F  E  N  S  O  I  A
M  R  N  S  P  N  A  W  R  N  A  M  H  I  S  I  T  C
N  O  J  I  M  I  S  S  E  T  I  Z  C  M  J  L  S  S
X  F  Z  R  E  U  E  Q  F  S  K  C  I  Q  R  O  E  I
A  E  B  R  T  Q  K  F  S  Y  I  V  R  O  X  R  R  D
P  D  Q  U  K  N  U  I  E  T  R  G  B  B  N  T  A  P
J  M  B  S  D  I  O  D  A  E  L  N  B  F  H  E  C  Q
I  D  N  E  C  N  I  T  R  O  P  S  A  R  T  P  T  C
Q  I  J  K  I  R  T  S  A  S  I  D  F  M  R  B  V  H
```

ALLUVIONI	EMISSIONI	MALATTIE
COMBUSTIBILI	EROSIONE	PETROLIO
CARBONE	ESALAZIONI	PRECIPITAZIONI
CARESTIA	ELETTRICITÀ	SICCITÀ
DEFORESTAZIONE	FERTILIZZANTI	SURRISCALDAMENTO
DESERTIFICAZIONE	INCENDI	SFRUTTAMENTO
DISASTRI	FABBRICHE	TEMPERATURA
DISCARICHE	INQUINAMENTO	TRASPORTI

Translate the English words below the grid into Italian and find them in the Word Search. If this is too challenging, please turn the page for an easier puzzle.

```
L  H  N  Y  Q  V  O  Q  O  B  Q  D  F  E  I
F  U  C  T  Y  D  O  A  S  O  N  A  R  F  R
A  F  S  A  T  A  V  E  N  N  I  S  S  I  A
A  R  P  S  A  T  E  T  N  E  N  O  P  M  I
S  Y  A  O  U  A  D  N  U  P  Y  I  S  S  G
S  X  I  I  A  R  C  A  G  M  D  C  A  V  G
A  D  V  B  S  O  E  I  X  A  E  C  S  Y  A
B  I  R  B  O  L  K  G  J  I  L  O  O  Z  V
K  A  E  E  R  P  T  G  G  S  I  R  U  A  L
K  S  P  N  T  S  S  E  W  I  B  Y  T  S  E
F  O  M  K  E  E  F  D  I  W  A  C  R  O  S
A  C  I  T  I  N  A  R  G  V  L  N  O  B  A
M  S  A  Y  P  I  T  E  R  V  A  I  T  R  S
B  O  Y  R  N  B  L  V  E  V  C  P  S  E  F
R  B  F  H  F  K  A  S  O  T  S  E  A  M  K
```

HIGH	UNEXPLORED	STONY
HARSH	INACCESSIBLE	STEEP
LOW	COMMANDING	ROCKY
WOODY	SNOWY	CLIMBABLE
GRASSY	LUSH	WILD
CRUMBLY	MAJESTIC	TORTUOUS
GRANITIC	MISTY	VERDANT

Aggettivi della montagna

Find the Italian words below the grid in the Word Search puzzle. These are the same Italian words as in 74a, but they're located in different positions on the grid.

```
N G A D I P I R W I V H R N A
B A S O U T R O T W D Z X Y I
A S O N A R F J D V U U H M G
T O C E V A S O R T E I P V G
L T S X K P T O X N M O E L A
A S O B R E C A S K N R M P V
J E B O M C K A V E D F W T L
C A S O I B B E N E D N K G E
J M B O C F F T G C N E S V S
L U S S U R E G G I A N T E S
I A R P S A I V R E P M I M S
Y T S F C A C I T I N A R G J
M R K S N N K X T V P Y O C S
K Z A T A R O L P S E N I J N
M J E L I B A L A C S G M I I
```

ALTA	INESPLORATA	PIETROSA
ASPRA	IMPERVIA	RIPIDA
BASSA	IMPONENTE	ROCCIOSA
BOSCOSA	INNEVATA	SCALABILE
ERBOSA	LUSSUREGGIANTE	SELVAGGIA
FRANOSA	MAESTOSA	TORTUOSA
GRANITICA	NEBBIOSA	VERDEGGIANTE

Luci e ombre

Translate the English words below the grid into Italian and find them in the Word Search. If this is too challenging, please turn the page for an easier puzzle.

```
L S A E L O S O N R O I G B G
O U B N R E T N E L K T O S W
M D M O P F K E T N E G R O S
B F N I E R O L O C O A T I P
R D A Z N E R A P S A R T G D
A N Z A O E E B Z O M B E G C
D P N R I N S O R C S M P A T
H Q E F S O A C Y C I O S R C
E X U I S T L R E L R N T G V
U A Q R E O H A R N P E V T Q
G H E I L F K L B Y Z P D M A
P G R H F Q X L E M P A Y X C
D U F A I G R E N E D I R I T
A L I Y R L I T E T T O N T I
M R S I M I J S T U J I M L C
```

RAINBOW	LENS	REFLECTION
COLOUR	LUMINESCENCE	REFRACTION
ENERGY	NIGHT	SUN
FREQUENCY	SHADOW	SOURCE
PHOTON	WAVE	SPECTRUM
DAY	HALF-LIGHT	STAR
IRIS	PRISM	DARKNESS
LASER	BEAM	TRANSPARENCY

Luci e ombre

Find the Italian words below the grid in the Word Search puzzle. These are the same Italian words as in 75a, but they're located in different positions on the grid.

```
A J E X U E N O I Z A R F I R
E Z P E T A Z N E U Q E R F E
E X E R X R K E T N E G R O S
K F J T I B M L R O U A E K A
I S O U T M T A L E Z R Q O L
U O A D N O U B E N O T O F G
W Z A C G N N O E O N R O I G
X M E T N E L C A I G R E N E
O R T T E P S R B S H X W H R
I B A Z N E R A P S A R T R B
G U R F N R Y M L E D I R I E
G L B I P O A S N L M M K V N
A K M H M L G I C F E L O S E
R U O C V O Q R Z I M T J L T
L O H W R C I P A R U S S M S
```

ARCOBALENO   LENTE   RIFLESSIONE
COLORE   LUMINESCENZA   RIFRAZIONE
ENERGIA   NOTTE   SOLE
FREQUENZA   OMBRA   SORGENTE
FOTONE   ONDA   SPETTRO
GIORNO   PENOMBRA   STELLA
IRIDE   PRISMA   TENEBRE
LASER   RAGGIO   TRASPARENZA

Continenti e oceani

This freeform crossword has the clues in Italian. If you struggle to understand some of the clues, you can find them in English in the *Help Section* on page 132

Orizzontali

4. Quando la nave affonda
6. L'oceano attraversato da Cristoforo Colombo
9. La Grande Barriera lunga 2,300 Km
11. L'oceano più piccolo della terra
12. Livello del mare che sale e scende

Verticali

1. L'oceano più grande del mondo
2. Il continente di cui fa parte l'Italia
3. Il continente più piccolo
5. Un continente al Polo Sud
7. Il continente dove vivono i leoni
8. Il continente più grande
10. Il Madagascar si trova in questo oceano

Piante e fiori

This freeform crossword has the clues in Italian. If you struggle to understand some of the clues, you can find them in English in the *Help Section* on page 132

Orizzontali

5. Crescono sotto terra
6. La scienza delle piante
8. Involucro esterno dell'albero
10. Lo raccolgono le api per fare il miele
11. Pigmento verde delle foglie

Verticali

1. Difesa della pianta
2. Un braccio dell'albero
3. Una parte della corolla
4. Il corpo dell'albero
6. Il fiore non ancora aperto
7. L'origine della pianta
9. Polvere gialla dei fiori

Cereali e derivati

The following words have been scrambled. Place the letters in the correct order.
For a less challenging version of this puzzle, please turn the page.

EAANV　　　_ _ _ _ _

ARFRO　　　_ _ _ _ _

RFETNMOU　　_ _ _ _ _ ___

IASM　　　_ _ _ _

IOGIML　　　_ _ _ _ _ _

ROZO　　　_ _ _ _

OSIR　　　_ _ _ _

EGSEAL　　　_ _ _ _ _ _

IARANF　　　_ _ _ _ _ _

MDOAI　　　_ _ _ _ _

MSOLAE　　　_ _ _ _ _ _

SACCUR　　　_ _ _ _ _ _

Cereali e derivati

The words on the left have been scrambled. Place the letters in the correct order.

EAANV   A _ _ _ _

ARFRO   F _ _ _ _

RFETNMOU   F _ _ _ _ _ O

IASM   M _ _ _

IOGIML   M _ _ _ _ _

ROZO   O _ _ _

OSIR   R _ _ _

EGSEAL   S _ _ _ _ E

IARANF   F _ _ _ _ A

MDOAI   A _ _ _ _

MSOLAE   S _ _ _ _ A

SACCUR   C _ _ _ _ A

Geografia dell'Italia

Find the Italian words below the grid in the Word Search puzzle.

```
K  R  A  E  O  G  F  D  J  C  X  D  Q  S  S
O  O  I  V  U  S  E  V  Q  P  I  P  T  Y  R
W  N  H  A  Z  X  A  Q  E  L  A  V  I  T  S
E  I  C  I  O  T  O  N  E  R  R  I  T  U  X
Q  C  S  P  I  N  I  N  N  E  P  P  A  I  S
W  I  I  C  N  S  F  I  P  C  N  L  K  T  P
M  T  A  O  O  G  O  U  L  O  P  A  C  L  B
R  N  A  L  I  C  B  E  N  O  I  G  E  R  U
O  U  A  B  K  B  J  J  P  C  T  R  B  V  U
P  L  T  I  L  O  B  M  O  R  T  S  P  Y  C
M  E  D  I  T  E  R  R  A  N  E  O  K  A  F
S  O  C  I  T  A  I  R  D  A  L  U  F  G  C
K  A  I  C  N  I  V  O  R  P  A  J  P  B  F
I  S  O  L  E  G  I  D  A  P  I  Z  G  J  F
V  H  V  V  K  J  O  H  G  T  D  P  V  K  O
```

ADIGE	GARDA	REGIONE
ADRIATICO	IONIO	REPUBBLICA
ALPI	ISCHIA	STIVALE
APPENNINI	ISOLE	STROMBOLI
CAPOLUOGO	MEDITERRANEO	TICINO
CAPRI	PENISOLA	TIRRENO
DIALETTI	PIAVE	VATICANO
ELBA	PROVINCIA	VESUVIO

L'atomo

Below this Word Fit puzzle there is a list of words.
Place the words correctly into the grid.

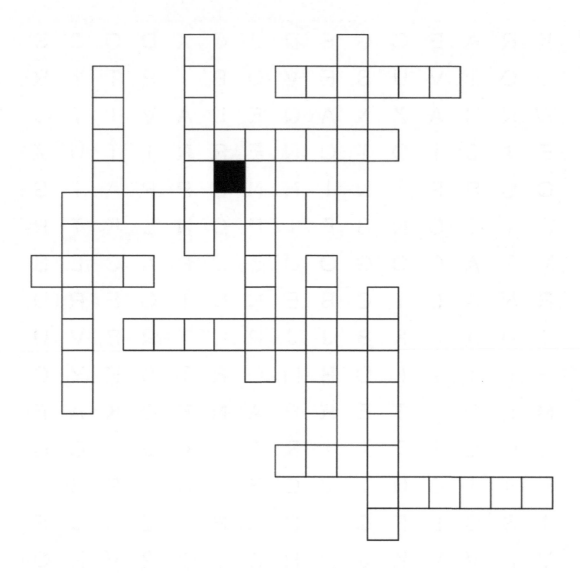

4 lettere
Ione
Moto

5 lettere
Massa

6 lettere
Carica
Nucleo
Orbita

7 lettere
Energia
Isotopo
Materia
Protone

8 lettere
Neutrone
Elemento

9 lettere
Elettrone

10 lettere
Particella

I biomi

Translate the English words below the grid into Italian and find them in the Word Search. If this is too challenging, please turn the page for an easier puzzle.

```
P  H  V  E  U  U  Y  P  H  B  D  E  Z  O  E  T
A  R  U  T  A  R  E  P  M  E  T  R  H  T  L  U
I  E  E  N  O  I  Z  A  T  E  G  E  V  N  C  Q
R  N  C  C  T  Y  L  E  E  A  C  I  A  E  M  M
E  I  M  S  I  N  A  G  R  O  R  C  I  M  T  S
T  D  R  A  P  P  E  T  S  H  O  E  H  A  U  P
A  U  I  M  C  D  I  I  J  N  I  P  C  T  K  G
R  T  N  I  V  R  S  T  I  O  R  S  C  T  U  X
P  I  O  L  X  T  M  F  A  D  O  M  A  A  Z  M
A  T  I  C  E  P  E  J  I  Z  T  J  M  D  O  F
N  A  G  M  W  R  E  T  N  E  I  B  M  A  A  S
A  L  A  R  E  F  S  O  I  B  R  O  P  U  Q  Y
V  D  T  G  I  U  N  G  L  A  R  D  N  U  T  U
A  T  S  E  R  O  F  H  K  N  E  A  G  I  A  T
S  S  J  E  P  D  C  K  W  O  T  R  E  S  E  D
V  L  E  E  O  G  S  X  Z  N  G  D  H  Z  K  A
```

ADAPTATION	FOREST	STEPPE
ENVIRONMENT	JUNGLE	SEASONS
BIOSPHERE	LATITUDE	SPECIES
CLIMATE	MAQUIS	TAIGA
CONIFERS	MICRO-ORGANISM	TEMPERATURE
ECOSYSTEM	GRASSLAND	TERRITORY
DESERT	PRECIPITATIONS	TUNDRA
FAUNA	SAVANNAH	VEGETATION

I biomi

Find the Italian words below the grid in the Word Search puzzle. These are the same Italian words as in 81a, but they're located in different positions on the grid.

```
P A M E T S I S O C E W N V D G
E R E F I N O C L R N R O O F I
I U E S M H A I N O I G A T S U
C T N C S L M B S H D S T R K N
E A O B I A S W S D U N S E I G
P R I J N P T S I F T F E S E L
S E Z E A O I R O T I R R E T A
Q P A A G I A T H G T Y O D N I
V M T F R O A N A V A S F A E H
Z E E U O Q N P I Z L B T I I C
P T G I R Q U G R D I H S D B C
Z T E A C N A R E F S O I B M A
T X V Y I G F A T M C K N E A M
O T N E M A T T A D A U U I L M
W B S C B N L A R D N U T P B E
K R Z B X Y D A P P E T S H E U
```

ADATTAMENTO	FORESTA	STEPPA
AMBIENTE	GIUNGLA	STAGIONI
BIOSFERA	LATITUDINE	SPECIE
CLIMA	MACCHIA	TAIGA
CONIFERE	MICRORGANISMI	TEMPERATURA
ECOSISTEMA	PRATERIA	TERRITORIO
DESERTO	PRECIPITAZIONI	TUNDRA
FAUNA	SAVANA	VEGETAZIONE

Terremoti, tsunami e vulcani

Translate the English words below the grid into Italian and find them in the Word Search. If this is too challenging, please turn the page for an easier puzzle.

```
A O U A A K L A Z N E T O P A
S L C W N Y U N O N N A D L S
V L I A T A D N O E O J O A S
O O J Z C N R I T F I J L Z O
E R E N E C Z F N O Z V O N C
R C N O T U C A E R A M C E S
E R O R R E T N M T U X I G S
E M I T T I V I A S C I R R L
L E S N E V V G G A A L E E S
A I O E D R G Z A T V L P M E
D I L C F I E R L A E I X E J
N R P I O F P T L C Y P M Q W
O Z S P V E M R A L L A S A Z
F F E E N O I Z U R E L H I A
X X O A T L T Y R S C R J E G
```

FLOODING	EMERGENCY	TIDE
ALERT	EPICENTRE	BIG WAVE
CATASTROPHE	ERUPTION	DANGER
ASH	EXPLOSION	POWER (MIGHT)
CRATER	EVACUATION	RESCUE
COLLAPSE	SEABED	TREMOR (SHOCK)
DAMAGE	LANDSLIDE	TERROR
DESTRUCTION	LAPILLI	CASUALTIES

Terremoti, tsunami e vulcani

Find the Italian words below the grid in the Word Search puzzle. These are the same Italian words as in 82a, but they're located in different positions on the grid.

```
E  F  O  R  T  S  A  T  A  C  D  K  B  J  A
N  N  X  I  F  W  X  K  H  F  I  P  A  L  L
O  L  O  C  I  R  E  P  O  C  S  Q  L  R  L
I  T  I  I  W  R  J  N  A  I  T  A  S  R  A
S  I  G  Q  Z  F  D  Z  G  C  R  Y  F  L  G
O  B  G  Y  O  A  J  N  R  M  U  E  A  S  A
L  F  A  N  L  Z  U  A  E  X  Z  P  L  C  M
P  K  T  E  L  N  T  C  R  E  I  Z  B  O  E
S  A  A  G  O  E  B  T  A  L  O  N  A  S  N
E  T  V  E  R  G  E  F  L  V  N  A  Z  S  T
R  A  L  E  C  R  T  I  B  H  E  E  N  A  O
E  D  A  N  R  E  N  O  I  Z  U  R  E  N  N
N  N  S  O  W  M  R  R  J  B  H  A  T  A  N
E  O  R  T  N  E  C  I  P  E  C  M  O  R  A
C  E  M  I  T  T  I  V  F  P  Z  F  P  F  D
```

ALLAGAMENTO	EMERGENZA	MAREA
ALLARME	EPICENTRO	ONDATA
CATASTROFE	ERUZIONE	PERICOLO
CENERE	ESPLOSIONE	POTENZA
CRATERE	EVACUAZIONE	SALVATAGGIO
CROLLO	FONDALE	SCOSSA
DANNO	FRANA	TERRORE
DISTRUZIONE	LAPILLI	VITTIME

Creature del mare e del fiume

Translate the English words below the grid into Italian and find them in the Word Search. If this is too challenging, please turn the page for an easier puzzle.

```
U R W O N Q E Q W V O O K Z J
Z I W I U I A O Q E R Z S O A
L Y N C O N O T C N A L P V P
W A B C F D B A A S U D E M R
S K C I T B T D A G U I C C A
P L B R J S F U S L A L P E C
L I V O O I H C N A R G L N V
A G U R A T R A T L T Y O O L
M X C C L E K R B L N C K I M
D E L F I N O R O I O D Q R V
Z T K J G O Y A F U L G H O I
Z K Z O D M D B Q G K S P T G
L P A N E L A B A N G U P S G
Z H A S Z A C O F A I P P E S
E X F P X S L V A M H W S I E
```

AMPHIBIA	DOLPHIN	PLANKTON
ANCHOVY	SEAL	SEA URCHIN
EEL	CRAB	SALMON
WHALE	OTTER	CUTTLEFISH
BARRACUDA	JELLYFISH	SPONGE
CARP	MOLLUSC	STURGEON
CRUSTACEAN	KILLER-WHALE	TURTLE

Creature del mare e del fiume

Find the Italian words below the grid in the Word Search puzzle. These are the same Italian words as in 83a, but they're located in different positions on the grid.

```
B F Y A F S E I G Q N D D E O
Q A L L I U G N A G U I C C A
M G R E Z H W W E J G S K Q N
O U L R C O C S U L L O M P E
L R E C A E N I A H X I G I L
H A N O T C N A L P K H Q J A
K T O N B A U B R H J C L B B
C R I I F T U D B P U N S N H
O A R F U S U N A P R A C Y S
B T O L A O Q F C Q L R I F G
S C T E S R Z O R M L G B N A
A V S D U C T Q O I C C I R J
Y G B R D N A N G U P S F J W
A I P P E S E S O H L N N J Y
U N Q C M K S A K L M R A E E
```

ANFIBI	DELFINO	PLANCTON
ACCIUGA	FOCA	RICCIO
ANGUILLA	GRANCHIO	SALMONE
BALENA	LONTRA	SEPPIA
BARRACUDA	MEDUSA	SPUGNA
CARPA	MOLLUSCO	STORIONE
CROSTACEO	ORCA	TARTARUGA

Geografia del mondo

This freeform crossword has the clues in Italian. If you struggle to understand some of the clues, you can find them in English in the *Help Section* on page 132

Orizzontali

4. Patria di Maradona

7. Il deserto più grande in Africa

8. Provincia canadese dove parlano il francese

11. La catena montuosa più alta del mondo

12. Famoso fiume dell'America

Verticali

1. L'isola più grande del mondo

2. L'isola più grande dei Caraibi

3. Promontorio roccioso a sud della Spagna

5. Il Paese dei Samurai

6. La catena montuosa più lunga della terra

9. Regione molto fredda della Russia

10. Lo Stato del monte Kilimanjaro

Discipline scientifiche

This freeform crossword has the clues in Italian. If you struggle to understand some of the clues, you can find them in English in the *Help Section* on page 133

Orizzontali

1. Lo studio del clima e sue variazioni
2. Studio dell'ambiente
6. Studio dei popoli antichi
8. Lo studio dei terremoti
10. Studio degli insetti
11. Studio dei numeri e delle misure

Verticali

1. Lo studio delle sostanze e come reagiscono
3. Studio degli organismi viventi
4. Ne erano esperti Newton e Einstein
5. Studio delle stelle e pianeti
7. Studio degli animali
9. Lo studio della struttura della Terra

Parti dell'albero e del frutto

Match the Italian words on the left, to the English words on the right.

tronco	peel
radici	bark
foglie	flowers
rami	pulp
chioma	leaves
corteccia	seeds
fiori	crown
semi	branches
picciolo	trunk
buccia	stalk
polpa	core
torsolo	roots

Gli elementi chimici più abbondanti sulla terra

Match the Italian words on the left, to the English words on the right.

ossigeno	sodium
silicio	phosphorus
alluminio	silicon
ferro	hydrogen
calcio	titanium
sodio	aluminium
potassio	manganese
magnesio	calcium
idrogeno	potassium
titanio	iron
fosforo	magnesium
manganese	oxygen

La crescita demografica

Below this Word Fit puzzle there is a list of words. Place the words correctly into the grid (treat the vowels with accents as ordinary vowels, inside the grid)

4 lettere
Dati

7 lettere
Densità

8 lettere
Abitanti
Natalità

9 lettere
Fertilità
Longevità
Mortalità

10 lettere
Incremento
Proiezioni

11 lettere
Popolazioni
Statistiche

13 lettere
Distribuzione

Animali ruminanti

The following words have been scrambled. Place the letters in the correct order.
For a less challenging version of this puzzle, please turn the page.

ELAC _ _ _ _

LPIATENO _ _ _ _ _ _ _ _

TAIREE _ _ _ _ _ _

EOBTSNI _ _ _ _ _ _ _

OBLUAF _ _ _ _ _ _

AIOCCSOM _ _ _ _ _ _ _ _

ZLLAEZGA _ _ _ _ _ _ _ _

AMALPI _ _ _ _ _ _

NONEMTO _ _ _ _ _ _ _

NMEOFUL _ _ _ _ _ _ _

ENNRA _ _ _ _ _

MSTOCACEB _ _ _ _ _ _ _ _ _

Animali ruminanti

The words on the left have been scrambled. Place the letters in the correct order.

ELAC   A _ _ _

LPIATENO   A _ _ _ L _ _ E

TAIREE   A _ _ _ _ E

EOBTSNI   B _ _ _ _ _ E

OBLUAF   B _ _ _ _ O

AIOCCSOM   C _ _ _ S _ _ O

ZLLAEZGA   G _ _ _ E _ _ A

AMALPI   I _ _ _ _ A

NONEMTO   M _ _ T _ _ E

NMEOFUL   M _ _ L _ _ _ E

ENNRA   R _ _ _ _

MSTOCACEB   S _ _ M _ _ _ _ O

Il mondo degli insetti

Translate the English words below the grid into Italian and find them in the Word Search. If this is too challenging, please turn the page for an easier puzzle.

```
B P L M O C A L L A F R A F O
H V P C X Y L L X W A V R A L
Y L U W G S A N U A N A W A R
H R E S O S C H E L E T R O A
B D N M E M I B M L L T Q I T
H Z N I B C C Y O E A E O E H
Q D E M A I C S D N F L B D C
D Z T P R L U C D I U L M I P
B B N O A A H J A C O A O T L
N I A M C E Y O C C Z V B N X
X Y T D S Z C I L O N A F A T
L Z T N Q O O A V C Y C O M I
H T A D O L L I R G T T T L G
B X L E A C I M R O F R C U Z
M K B O Z K T F Z D T O I D C
```

ABDOMEN	CICADA	DRAGONFLY
WINGS	LADYBIRD	FIREFLY
ANTENNAE	EXOSKELETON	MANTIS
BEE	MOTH	BEETLE
COCKROACH	BUTTERFLY	SWARM
BUMBLEBEE	ANT	HORSEFLY
CATERPILLAR	CRICKET	WOODWORM
GRASSHOPPER	LARVA	THORAX

Il mondo degli insetti

Find the Italian words below the grid in the Word Search puzzle. These are the same Italian words as in 90a, but they're located in different positions on the grid.

```
E  F  I  S  S  F  U  D  W  G  S  P  N  Q  X
M  A  V  R  A  L  I  A  C  I  M  R  O  F  V
O  S  S  L  Z  X  O  L  L  I  R  G  N  O  P
D  C  E  R  R  J  N  O  E  B  A  R  A  C  S
D  N  Z  J  U  E  D  I  T  N  A  M  F  U  R
A  L  L  E  N  I  C  C  O  C  E  P  A  R  O
T  R  W  O  N  C  A  C  N  I  C  W  T  B  B
T  X  T  H  Y  N  A  U  O  S  A  S  U  L  M
E  S  O  S  C  H  E  L  E  T  R  O  A  Y  O
L  B  W  J  V  J  G  T  F  E  O  T  L  U  B
L  N  R  O  J  F  V  T  N  M  T  A  A  B  O
A  L  U  L  L  E  B  I  L  A  L  A  C  S  Y
V  O  W  R  V  N  V  V  G  I  P  R  I  C  D
A  L  L  A  F  R  A  F  Z  C  R  T  C  B  I
C  Y  H  T  V  N  I  W  F  S  Z  Q  N  R  X
```

ADDOME	CICALA	LIBELLULA
ALI	COCCINELLA	LUCCIOLA
ANTENNE	ESOSCHELETRO	MANTIDE
APE	FALENA	SCARABEO
BLATTA	FARFALLA	SCIAME
BOMBO	FORMICA	TAFANO
BRUCO	GRILLO	TARLO
CAVALLETTA	LARVA	TORACE

Alcuni fiori

Translate the English words below the grid into Italian and find them in the Word Search. If this is too challenging, please turn the page for an easier puzzle.

```
C A O L O C N U N A R J G Z O
S R N B F Q C P E O N I A E R
H T I W W A R E B R E G S D T
H S M S M W X R L R D S A H E
D E A E A L U N A P M A C G N
T N L O T N A P A G A C L O S
R I C W I L T R A I L A D Z I
A G I O R D N E D O D O R Z A
L K C N E D B Y M I O V E G T
U E I A H E X Z O O N T N T T
M Y H F G T U L I P A N O M E
I X A O R D O C S I B I M L L
R R N R A E D I H C R O E C O
P I T A M B N I Y I W Y N Z I
A R Z G I W F X S S T D A Y V
```

AGAPANTHUS	CARNATION	HYDRANGEA
ANEMONE	GLADIOLUS	ORCHID
BEGONIA	GERBERA	PEONY
CAMELLIA	BROOM	PRIMROSE
BELLFLOWER	HIBISCUS	BUTTERCUP
CYCLAMEN	IRIS	RHODODENDRON
CHRYSANTHEMUM	LOTUS	TULIP
DAHLIA	DAISY	VIOLET

Alcuni fiori

Find the Italian words below the grid in the Word Search puzzle. These are the same Italian words as in 91a, but they're located in different positions on the grid.

```
Q A I Q B P Z L D E R Q I C T
X F Q K E M U A I S N E T R O
S S H O N A F O R A G E K I M
R S N L O A I N O A T B A S O
F I E O M A T I R E H G R A M
A R A I E L W M D D T O T N B
I I H D N U K A N I E N S T A
L H K A A N G L E H E A E E L
A W X L L A M C D C E P N M U
D S D G P P A I O R B I I O M
O T Y A F M J C D O V L G Y I
E K N Z E A O L O C N U N A R
O T O L D C J C R C L T D S P
O V I O L E T T A R E B R E G
B A I N O G E B I B I S C O M
```

AGAPANTO   GAROFANO   ORTENSIA
ANEMONE   GLADIOLO   ORCHIDEA
BEGONIA   GERBERA   PEONIA
CAMELIA   GINESTRA   PRIMULA
CAMPANULA   IBISCO   RANUNCOLO
CICLAMINO   IRIS   RODODENDRO
CRISANTEMO   LOTO   TULIPANO
DALIA   MARGHERITA   VIOLETTA

Translate the English words below the grid into Italian and find them in the Word Search. If this is too challenging, please turn the page for an easier puzzle.

```
C H B L P S Y Z T H H P G W A
C R E F H G O V E V Z K J L C
A A I B B I B O I P M E T Q J
P O M S I U D N I O C A C E P
A O E A T E F O R P R S Y C C
V M E N O I Z A R E N E V O E
S S Q B M Z A R E I H G E R P
I I O J S A O N A R O C I C E
N O M S I A R B E R I T R A M
A A L L E P P A C S O F J A A
G T M P T B Q A S E I H C L L
O B O L O P E C S I D M A F S
G P O T N A S A E H C S O M I
A X I K O M S I E T I L O P S
S M D O M S I D D U B H B Z N
```

ALTAR	DISCIPLE	PRAYER
BIBLE	JUDAISM	PROPHET
BUDDHISM	HINDUISM	RITE
CHAPEL	ISLAM	SAINT
CHURCH	MARTYR	SYNAGOGUE
KORAN	MONOTHEISM	TAOISM
CHRISTIANITY	MOSQUE	TEMPLE
CROSS	POLYTHEISM	WORSHIP

Religioni del mondo e parole relative

Find the Italian words below the grid in the Word Search puzzle. These are the same Italian words as in 92a, but they're located in different positions on the grid.

```
Q P U J Z F B S E C X C I C B
U D O R E I I O N H K R J O A
O E M J B N J M X I O I K R W
J T S B A U O S D E M S O A T
U Z I G A X M I G S S T M N N
E A O R L E S E Z A I I S O F
R G A A L C I T K A A A I T V
A A T P E O E I A R R N U N A
T Z Z P P R T L J E B E D A O
L O O D P C O O E I E S N S Y
A L Q L A J N P R H K I I E K
O A E H C S O M J G S M F S V
I S L A M L M A T E F O R P O
B U D D I S M O E R I T R A M
G L E A C O P O I P M E T D G
```

ALTARE
BIBBIA
BUDDISMO
CAPPELLA
CHIESA
CORANO
CRISTIANESIMO
CROCE

DISCEPOLO
EBRAISMO
INDUISMO
ISLAM
MARTIRE
MONOTEISMO
MOSCHEA
POLITEISMO

PREGHIERA
PROFETA
RITO
SANTO
SINAGOGA
TAOISMO
TEMPIO
VENERAZIONE

Alcuni Stati dell'Africa

The following words have been scrambled. Place the letters in the correct order.
For a less challenging version of this puzzle, please turn the page.

EIGAALR   _ _ _ _ _ _ _

GAALNO   _ _ _ _ _ _

NBRUIUD   _ _ _ _ _ _ _

MUCEARN   _ _ _ _ _ _ _

IPATOEI   _ _ _ _ _ _ _

AAGIBM   _ _ _ _ _ _

YNKEA   _ _ _ _ _

UAAIARTNMI   _ _ _ _ _ _ _ _ _ _

CAORCOM   _ _ _ _ _ _ _

CBMMOAZOI   _ _ _ _ _ _ _ _ _

AIGIENR   _ _ _ _ _ _ _

ATANNAZI   _ _ _ _ _ _ _ _

Alcuni Stati dell'Africa

The words on the left have been scrambled. Place the letters in the correct order.

EIGAALR   A _ _ _ _ A

GAALNO   A _ _ _ A

NBRUIUD   B _ _ U _ _ I

MUCEARN   C _ _ E _ _ N

IPATOEI   E _ _ _ _ _ A

AAGIBM   G _ _ _ _ A

YNKEA   K _ _ _ _

UAAIARTNMI   M _ _ _ I _ _ _ _ A

CAORCOM   M _ _ _ _ _ O

CBMMOAZOI   M _ _ _ M _ _ _ O

AIGIENR   N _ _ _ _ _ A

ATANNAZI   T _ _ Z _ _ _ A

Animali inverterbrati

This freeform crossword has the clues in Italian. If you struggle to understand some of the clues, you can find them in English in the *Help Section* on page 133

Orizzontali

3. Crostaceo che cammina di lato
6. È lungo, senza zampe e striscia
8. Futura farfalla
9. Elegante insetto con quattro ali
10. Insetto che canta
12. Piccolo insetto laborioso

Verticali

1. Ragno peloso e velenoso
2. Delizioso mollusco bivalve
4. Ha un corpo trasparente e vive nel mare
5. Ha tantissime zampette
7. Ha otto tentacoli
11. Mollusco molto lento

Bandiere del mondo

This freeform crossword has the clues in Italian. If you struggle to understand some of the clues, you can find them in English in the *Help Section* on page 133

Orizzontali

4. Ha la stella di David blu su sfondo bianco

6. È rossa con cinque stelle gialle

8. È rossa con una stella verde al centro

9. È bianca al centro con la foglia d'acero rossa

11. Ha una croce blu sul sfondo bianco

12. Ha tre bande orizzontali: nero, rosso e oro

Verticali

1. Ha una croce gialla su sfondo azzurro

2. È rossa con una luna e stella bianche

3. Ha tre bande verticali: blu, bianco e rosso

5. Ha due bande orizzontali: azzurro in alto e giallo in basso

7. Ha tre bande verticali: verde, bianco e rosso

10. Ha un disco rosso su sfondo bianco

Aggettivi del deserto

Translate the English words below the grid into Italian and find them in the Word Search. If this is too challenging, please turn the page for an easier puzzle.

```
R  Z  B  L  O  S  O  S  O  I  D  I  S  N  I
U  O  Y  M  I  V  O  P  D  O  S  E  T  S  E
U  O  D  I  R  A  S  E  L  I  B  O  M  M  I
W  C  U  O  A  E  O  T  A  L  O  S  E  D  Y
U  C  B  T  T  L  I  T  C  G  T  O  V  R  Q
I  E  I  A  I  A  Z  A  H  O  O  N  Y  E  O
N  S  B  T  L  T  N  C  J  P  M  I  S  N  T
C  R  T  I  O  I  E  O  F  S  E  M  D  D  I
O  L  Z  B  S  P  L  L  D  T  R  U  Y  V  N
L  F  U  A  N  S  I  A  O  N  L  L  E  M  I
T  V  L  S  U  O  S  R  V  A  A  N  W  G  F
O  B  D  I  Z  N  R  E  T  J  T  B  O  G  N
M  P  W  D  H  I  I  O  T  O  U  V  B  P  I
T  V  Z  B  D  Z  C  O  S  O  I  B  B  A  S
V  T  I  O  T  A  L  O  S  I  J  U  Y  P  D
```

ABANDONED	INFINITE	DRY
ARID	INHOSPITABLE	SILENT
HOT	DANGEROUS	SOLITARY
DESOLATE	ISOLATED	SPECTACULAR
UNINHABITED	BRIGHT	BARE
VAST	UNDULATING	SCORCHING
STILL	REMOTE	WINDY
UNCULTIVATED	SANDY	EMPTY

Aggettivi del deserto

Find the Italian words below the grid in the Word Search puzzle. These are the same Italian words as in 96a, but they're located in different positions on the grid.

```
N P I V A O T A L O S E D E E
C X O O D I R R O T R D A S I
O I L G O P S E C A N S M T N
S I N C O L T O L T O C C E S
O I R A T I L O S I R K W S L
I P X C C S C T P B B H O O D
Z E L V Y A H A I A I O M T O
N T L O T S O N X S S S M O S
E L A T I P S O N I O O N M O
L X E I O I O D R D L N G E I
I P P N D K T N A N A I N R B
S I E I I N N A D D T M J X B
S F O F R S E B O T O U V H A
O S V N A I V B L O D L A C S
O Y P I M O T A L U D N O D G
```

ABBANDONATO   INFINITO   SECCO
ARIDO   INOSPITALE   SILENZIOSO
CALDO   INSIDIOSO   SOLITARIO
DESOLATO   ISOLATO   SPETTACOLARE
DISABITATO   LUMINOSO   SPOGLIO
ESTESO   ONDULATO   TORRIDO
IMMOBILE   REMOTO   VENTOSO
INCOLTO   SABBIOSO   VUOTO

Translate the English words below the grid into Italian and find them in the Word Search. If this is too challenging, please turn the page for an easier puzzle.

```
S G P S M V A I O L O U B Q E
I C A Z N E U L F N I S S Q Q
F O I S O L O C R E B U T Z D
I L S E T I L E I M O I L O P
L E O T L R S C A B B I A L X
I R D I E A O N A T E T S L Y
D A I L S A L E P C T F A I R
E Y D A S I T T N R I M L B V
T J N F O D L I A T R Z L R E
I Z A E T I G N I N E M E O W
T L C C R M I O L B T R C M J
A Z X N E A N M O H F Z I C Y
P B D E P L U L S D I A R T E
E P V H S C A O O W D O A K E
M A L A R I A P R J D I V O C
```

AIDS
CANDIDIASIS
CHLAMYDIA
CHOLERA
COVID
DIPHTERIA
EBOLA
ENCEPHALITIS

HEPATITIS
GASTROENTERITIS
INFLUENZA
MALARIA
MENINGITIS
MEASLES
WHOOPING COUGH
POLIO

PNEUMONIA
RUBELLA
SCABIES
SYPHILIS
TETANUS
TUBERCULOSIS
SMALLPOX
CHICKENPOX

Malattie infettive

Find the Italian words below the grid in the Word Search puzzle. These are the same
Italian words as in 97a, but they're located in different positions on the grid.

```
S  I  F  I  L  I  D  E  A  G  X  Q  W  Y  Z
Z  E  H  S  U  A  I  B  B  A  C  S  D  I  A
E  T  I  R  E  T  F  I  D  S  A  L  O  B  E
S  I  P  S  Z  M  Z  F  N  T  I  O  I  F  K
S  T  I  E  O  A  W  E  E  R  D  L  S  V  S
O  A  E  T  I  L  E  I  M  O  I  L  O  P  C
T  P  T  I  Z  L  O  F  A  E  M  I  D  D  O
R  E  I  N  O  E  N  C  I  N  A  B  I  J  V
E  V  L  O  L  C  A  Q  R  T  L  R  D  R  I
P  B  A  M  O  I  T  G  A  E  C  O  N  O  D
C  O  F  L  I  R  E  F  L  R  B  M  A  S  U
D  G  E  O  A  A  T  B  A  I  A  U  C  O  W
Y  R  C  P  V  V  L  N  M  T  O  R  T  L  C
A  Z  N  E  U  L  F  N  I  E  X  A  U  I  Q
S  R  E  T  I  G  N  I  N  E  M  S  Z  A  W
```

AIDS	EPATITE	POLMONITE
CANDIDOSI	GASTROENTERITE	ROSOLIA
CLAMIDIA	INFLUENZA	SCABBIA
COLERA	MALARIA	SIFILIDE
COVID	MENINGITE	TETANO
DIFTERITE	MORBILLO	TUBERCOLOSI
EBOLA	PERTOSSE	VAIOLO
ENCEFALITE	POLIOMELITE	VARICELLA

The following words have been scrambled. Place the letters in the correct order.
For a less challenging version of this puzzle, please turn the page.

BAAL   _ _ _ _

UORAAR   _ _ _ _ _ _

UCLE   _ _ _ _

OSEL   _ _ _ _

TMTANIO   _ _ _ _ _ _ _

GIOPOEGRMI   _ _ _ _ _ _ _ _ _ _

ASER   _ _ _ _

OTORTMAN   _ _ _ _ _ _ _ _

RUOCCULEPS   _ _ _ _ _ _ _ _ _ _

OIUB   _ _ _ _

AUNL   _ _ _ _

ELSLET   _ _ _ _ _ _

Il giorno e la notte

The words on the left have been scrambled. Place the letters in the correct order.

BAAL   A _ _ _

UORAAR   A _ _ _ A

UCLE   L _ _ _

OSEL   S _ _ _

TMTANIO   M _ _ T _ _ O

GIOPOEGRMI   P _ _ _ _ I _ _ _ O

ASER   S _ _ _

OTORTMAN   T _ _ M _ _ _ O

RUOCCULEPS   C _ _ _ U _ _ _ _ _ O

OIUB   B _ _ _

AUNL   L _ _ _

ELSLET   S _ _ _ _ E

Il mondo dell'agricoltura

Translate the English words below the grid into Italian and find them in the Word Search. If this is too challenging, please turn the page for an easier puzzle.

```
F U P Z D S E M I C N O C R C
I E N O I Z A G I R R I H K P
A N R X W B L U M U F L A D R
N O A T L O C C A R Y G O P Q
G I O N I D A T N O C O T B P
J Z N W L L D A E M P M E V F
M U E P A F I O Y O F R N W N
E D R X E A C Z T A B E G D I
N O R X R I I A Z A M G I A G
S R E A E M T L C A R X V L G
L P T G C U S C F C N B E A A
W R G N R G E E R O T T A R T
O R B A T E P A P P A Z E R R
Z S K V G L F I W M O Q B E O
X V A T S Q D O E S W V H S T
```

PLOUGH	IRRIGATION	HARVEST
CEREALS	LEGUMES	GREENHOUSE
FERTILIZER (1)	MANURE	SOIL
FARMER	VEGETABLES	TRACTOR
WEEDS	PESTICIDE	SPADE
FERTILIZER (2)	PRUNING	HOE
SPROUT	PRODUCE	VINEYARD

Il mondo dell'agricoltura

Find the Italian words below the grid in the Word Search puzzle. These are the same Italian words as in 99a, but they're located in different positions on the grid.

```
F  P  O  T  E  N  G  I  V  A  S  O  R  Q  G
X  E  N  O  I  Z  A  G  I  R  R  I  C  D  D
Z  N  R  U  O  X  A  G  N  A  V  L  W  A  O
F  O  R  T  N  E  Z  A  Y  I  A  G  L  N  D
I  I  A  D  I  C  I  T  S  E  P  O  C  I  Z
H  Z  T  A  D  L  I  R  O  R  P  M  Y  H  H
H  U  L  Z  A  X  I  O  A  O  A  R  E  F  Z
G  D  O  R  T  U  Z  Z  P  T  Z  E  O  T  O
M  O  C  G  N  O  T  X  Z  T  W  G  N  C  G
P  R  C  I  O  R  E  C  C  A  B  R  E  E  N
I  P  A  M  C  T  D  P  D  R  N  R  R  W  C
Q  A  R  U  T  A  T  O  P  T  E  T  R  F  Z
O  S  H  G  F  R  T  E  V  A  R  R  E  S  S
J  E  V  E  M  A  T  E  L  J  I  N  T  O  L
V  U  P  L  Q  E  M  I  C  N  O  C  B  B  S
```

ARATRO	IRRIGAZIONE	RACCOLTA
CEREALI	LEGUMI	SERRA
CONCIME	LETAME	TERRENO
CONTADINO	ORTAGGI	TRATTORE
ERBACCE	PESTICIDA	VANGA
FERTILIZZANTE	POTATURA	ZAPPA
GERMOGLIO	PRODUZIONE	VIGNETO

In cerca di funghi

Below this Word Fit puzzle there is a list of words.
Place the words correctly into the grid.

5 lettere
Ovoli
Spore

7 lettere
Cestino
Porcini
Tartufi

8 lettere
Chiodini
Raccolta
Velenosi

9 lettere
Micologia
Prataioli

10 lettere
Sottobosco

12 lettere
Commestibili

Freeform Crosswords – Clues in English

3 – Insetti antipatici

Across

4. Unpleasant scalp parasite

7. Plant parasites

9. It resembles a bee but doesn't make honey

11. It has a very painful sting

12. Super tiny flying insect

Down

1. It can live in beds and it sucks blood

2. It likes to eat wood

3. It has long antennae and it's also called a cockroach

5. A grasshopper that destroys crops

6. It can cause malaria

8. It torments cats and dogs

10. Small winged insect, usually black

4 – Disastri naturali

Across

1. A submarine earthquake

6. It flows from the volcano

8. Large mass of snow that falls down

9. A prolonged period of no rainfall

10. When the ground shakes under your feet

11. A destructive, violent fire

Down

2. It caused dinosaurs to become extinct

3. It hit New Orleans in 2005 and was called Katrina

4. A violent wind storm that spins around

5. It worried Noah when he was building the ark

7. Earth and rocks falling down the mountain

15 – Animali carnivori

Across

2. I can scare the sheep

6. It jumps and lives by the pond

7. Huge snake that squeezes its prey

9. Web weaver

11. The king of the jungle

12. Bird that eats the flesh of dead animals

Down

1. Huge reptile with strong jaws

3. A feline that you keep at home

4. Largest sea mammal

5. A bird that lives in Antarctica

8. A large bird of prey that flies elegantly

10. Ferocious sea predator

16 – Animali erbivori

Across

6. Quadruped with very long neck
7. Farm animal with small beard
8. It lives in the desert and drinks a lot of water
10. Huge animal with long trunk
11. Fluffy small animal with long ears

Down

1. It makes the milk that is drunk the most
2. The largest ape
3. It has black and white stripes
4. The Trojan one was made of wood
5. A very slow reptile
8. A ruminant with antlers
9. Pack animal that is also stubborn

27 – Animali della fattoria

Across

3. Source of ham
6. It wakes everyone up at dawn
8. It lays one egg each day
9. Its ears are longer than a horse's
11. Messenger bird
12. Man's best friend

Down

1. The bird that gobbles
2. The black one is rare
4. It follows mother hen
5. It likes to hunt mice
7. It has webbed feet
10. Honey maker

28 – Fiumi del mondo

Across

3. It flows under London Bridge
5. A very long river in central Europe
7. The deepest river in the world
9. A famous river in Egypt
10. A very long river in South America
11. It flows in Paris

Down

1. A well-known river in Russia
2. The longest river in the United States
3. Rome's river
4. The longest river in Italy
6. It flows under Ponte Vecchio
8. A sacred river in India

39 – Alcune capitali

Across

2. Capital of China
5. Capital of Kenya
6. Capital of The Bahamas
9. Capital of Indonesia
10. Capital of Italy
11. Capital of the United Kingdom
12. Capital of Albania

Down

1. Capital of Poland
3. Capital of Australia
4. Capital of the United States
7. Capital of Sweden
8. Capital of Canada

40 – Il pianeta Terra

Across

2. Imaginary vertical line between the North Pole and the South Pole
4. The outer layer of the earth
9. Height above sea level
10. The motion of the earth around the sun
12. The layer of gases that surrounds the earth

Down

1. The earth does one each day
3. The largest rainforest
5. It divides the earth in two hemispheres (north and south)
6. Small island shaped like a doughnut
7. The air that we breathe
8. The colour of Earth seen from Space
11. The force that causes things to fall down

51 – Geografia dell'Italia

Across

3. Island of the Mar di Sicilia
6. The city of *gianduiotto* chocolate
7. Island south of Corsica
8. It's also called *La Serenissima*
9. The heel of Italy boot
10. The city of Romeo and Juliet

Down

1. Mountain range of the Alps
2. A big lake in Italy
4. St Francis' birthplace
5. The sea of Abruzzo
9. The largest plain in Italy
11. The volcano over Catania

52 – Che tempo fa?

Across

2. It melts when it rains
7. Weather science
9. Tropical winds that bring heavy rain
10. The amount of moisture in the air
11. A scale for measuring temperature
12. Hot wind from Africa

Down

1. It measures air pressure
3. It measures temperature
4. Electrical discharge during a storm
5. Small drops of water on the grass, in the morning
6. Rain made of small ice balls
8. Predictions about the weather

63 – Monumenti e luoghi spettacolari

Across

3. The Country of Taj Mahal
5. Egyptian royal tombs
7. The Country with the longest wall in the world
8. The State of the Golden Gate Bridge
10. A European capital famous for the Big Ben
11. Tuscan city with a leaning tower
12. Megalithic monument in Wiltshire

Down

1. The civilization that built Machu Picchu
2. Famous falls between Canada and United States
4. The most popular tower in Paris
6. Citadel over Athens
9. The largest amphitheatre in the world

64 – L'inquinamento

Across

4. Vehicles that come and go
6. Discarded materials
8. When a species ceases to exist
10. It screens the earth from ultraviolet rays
11. Synonym for poisonous and harmful
12. Chernobyl disaster had dangerous ones

Down

1. Material for water bottles
2. They're used in agriculture against pests
3. Global warming makes them melt
5. A fighter for the environment
7. Odourless and flammable gas
9. It pollutes the air in large cities

76 – Continenti e oceani

Across

4. When the ship sinks
6. The ocean crossed by Columbus
9. The Great Barrier, 2,300 Km long
11. The smallest ocean on earth
12. Sea level that goes up and down

Down

1. The largest ocean on earth
2. The continent Italy is part of
3. The smallest continent in the world
5. A continent on the South Pole
7. The continent where lions live
8. The largest continent in the world
10 Madagascar is in this ocean

77 – Piante e fiori

Across

5. They grow under the ground
6. The science of plants
8. It covers the outside of a tree
10. Bees collect it to make honey
11. Green pigment of plants

Down

1. A plant's defence
2. An arm of a tree
3. Corolla leaf
4. The main body of a tree
6. Unopened flower
7. The origin of a plant
9. Yellow powder from flowers

84 – Geografia del mondo

Across

4. The country of Maradona
7. The largest desert in Africa
8. French-speaking Canadian province
11. The highest mountain range in the world
12. Famous long river of North America

Down

1. The largest island in the world
2. The largest island in the Caribbean
3. Rocky peninsula in the south of Spain
5. The country of Samurai
6. The longest mountain range on earth
9. Extremely cold region in Russia
10. The country of Mount Kilimanjaro

85 – Discipline scientifiche

Across

1. The study of climate and how it varies
2. Environmental science
6. The study of peoples of the past
8. The study of earthquakes
10. The study of insects
11. The study of numbers and measures

Down

1. The study of substances and how they react
3. The study of living things
4. Newton and Einstein were experts in it
5. The study of stars and planets
7. The study of animals
9. The study of the structure of the Earth

94 – Animali invertebrati

Across

3. Crustacean that moves sideways
6. It's long, has no legs and it wiggles
8. A future butterfly
9. Elegant insect with four wings
10. Singing insect
12. Hard working small insect

Down

1. Hairy and poisonous spider
2. A delicious shellfish
4. It has a clear body and lives in the sea
5. Creature with lots of legs
7. It has eight tentacles
11. Very slow mollusc

95 – Bandiere del mondo

Across

4. It has a blue Star of David on a white background
6. It's red with five yellow stars
8. It's red with a green star in the centre
9. It has a white centre with a red maple leaf
11. It has a blue cross on a white field
12. It has three horizontal stripes: black, red and gold

Down

1. It has a yellow cross over a blue field
2. It's red with a white moon and star
3. It has three vertical bands: blue, white and red
5. It has two horizontal bands: blue at the top and yellow at the bottom
7. It has three vertical bands: green, white and red
10. It has a central red disk on a white field

Word Search Solutions

1a – Alcuni alberi

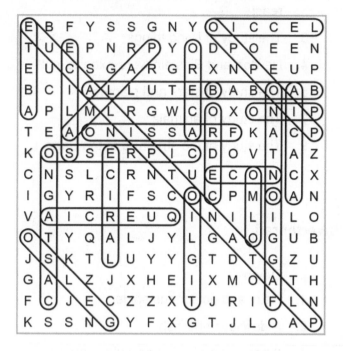

1b – Alcuni alberi

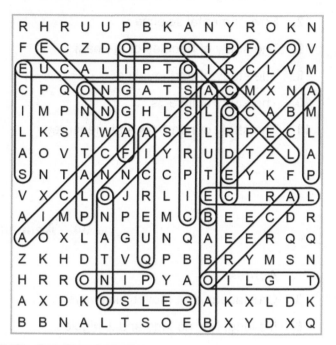

2a – Alcuni mammiferi

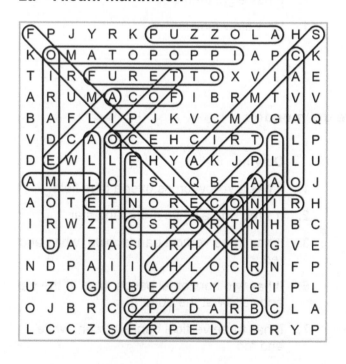

2b – Alcuni mammiferi

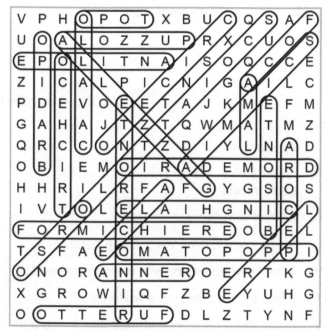

12a – Animali notturni

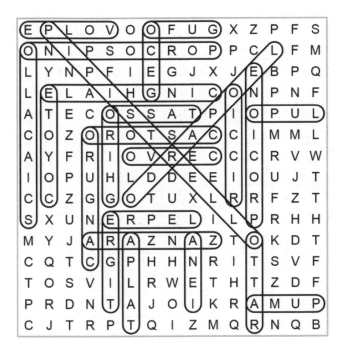

12b – Animali notturni

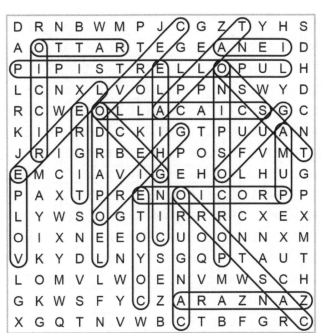

13a – Alcuni Stati del mondo

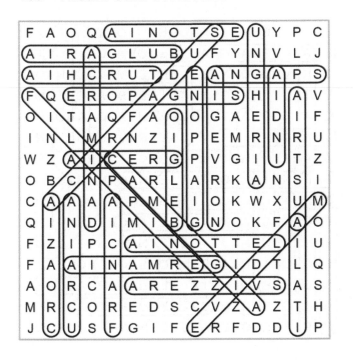

13b – Alcuni Stati del mondo

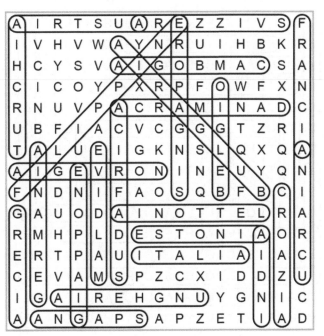

14a – L'Universo e lo Spazio

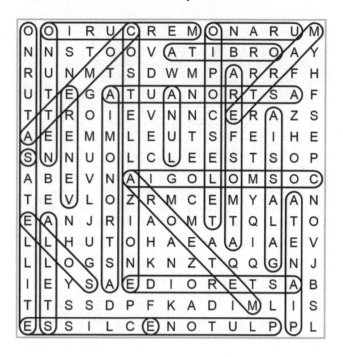

14b – L'Universo e lo Spazio

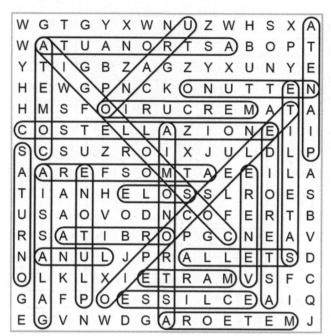

24a – Alcuni uccelli

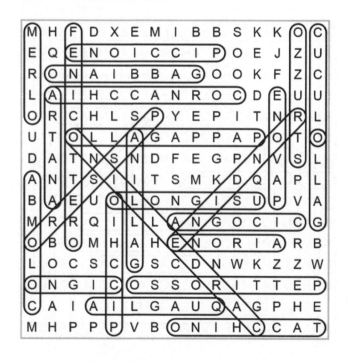

24b – Alcuni uccelli

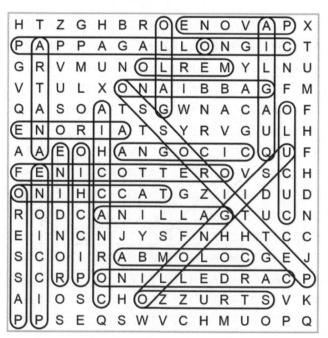

25a – Metalli e leghe

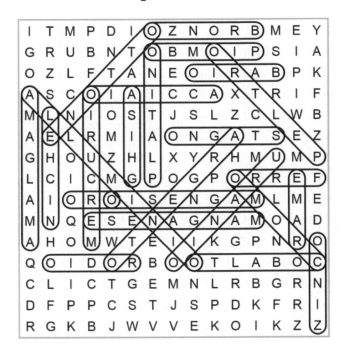

25b – Metalli e leghe

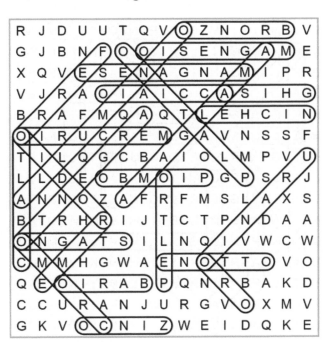

26a – I colori nella natura: Rosso

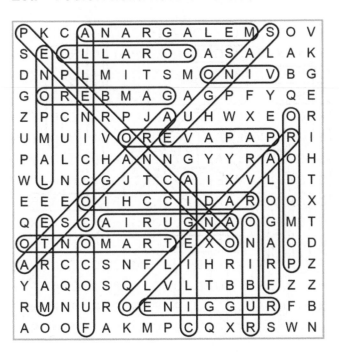

26b – I colori nella natura: Rosso

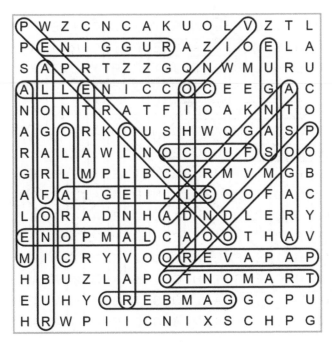

36a – I colori nella natura: Giallo

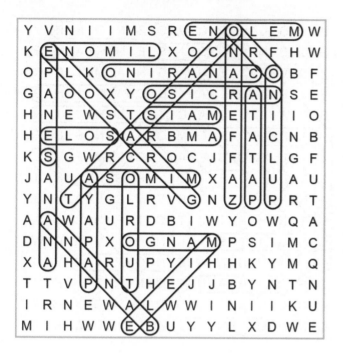

36b – I colori nella natura: Giallo

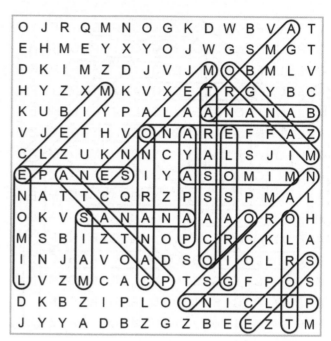

37a – Il mappamondo 1

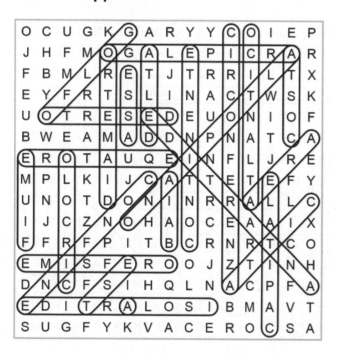

37b – Il mappamondo 1

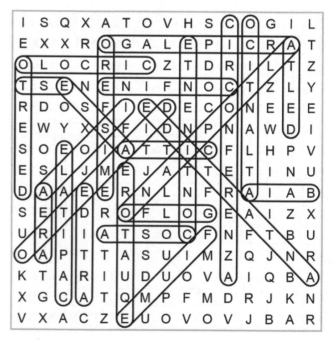

38a – Il mappamondo 2

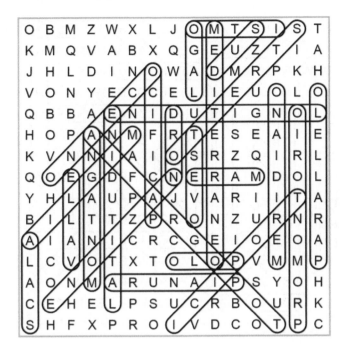

38b – Il mappamondo 2

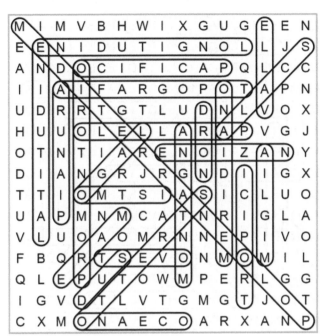

48a – Aggettivi del mare/oceano

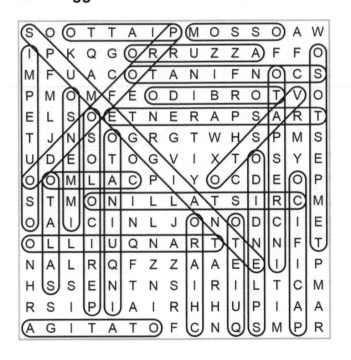

48b – Aggettivi del mare/oceano

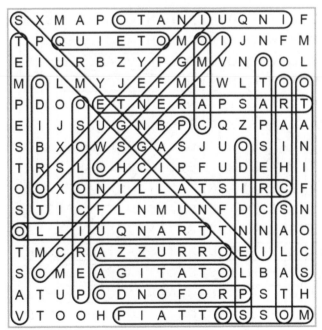

49a – I colori nella natura: Verde

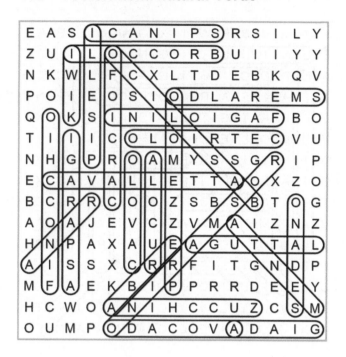

49b – I colori nella natura: Verde

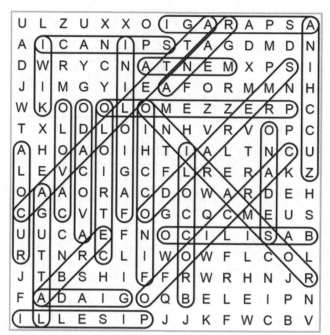

50a – Geologia

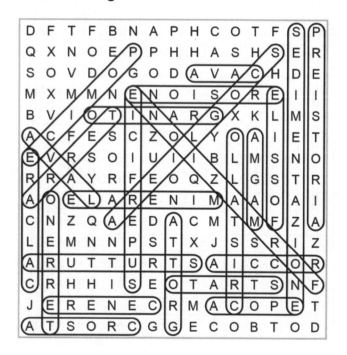

50b – Geologia

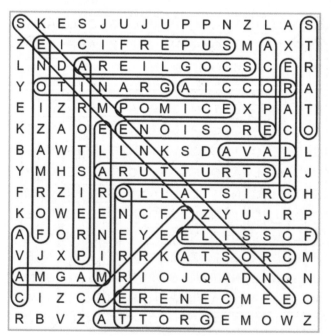

60a – Pietre preziose e gemme

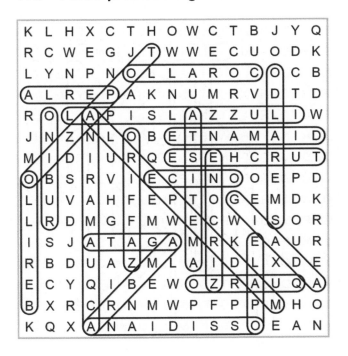

60b – Pietre preziose e gemme

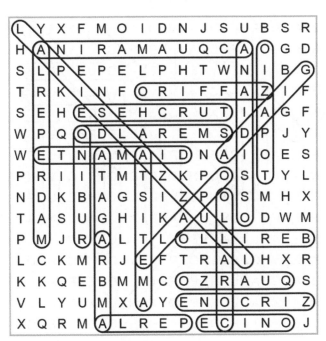

61a – Il mondo dei rettili e degli anfibi

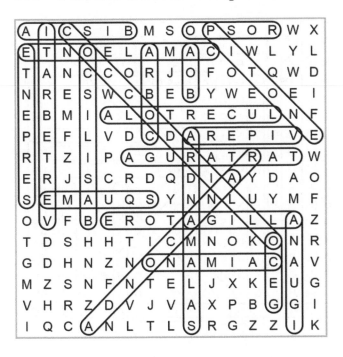

61b – Il mondo dei rettili e degli anfibi

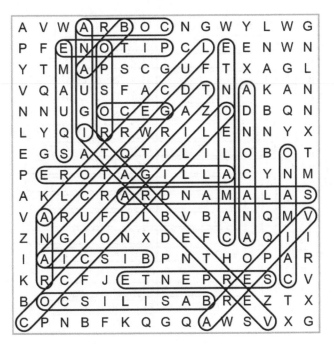

62a – I colori nella natura: Bianco

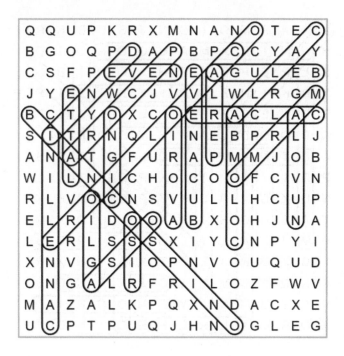

62b – I colori nella natura: Bianco

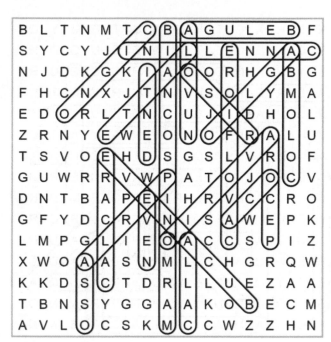

73a – Cambiamento climatico

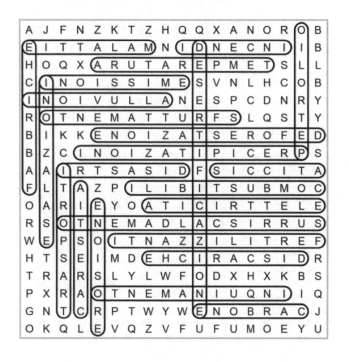

73b – Cambiamento climatico

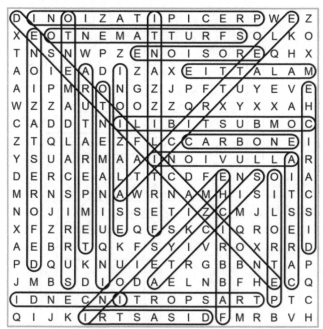

74a – Aggettivi della montagna

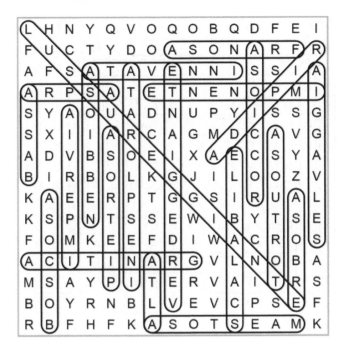

74b – Aggettivi della montagna

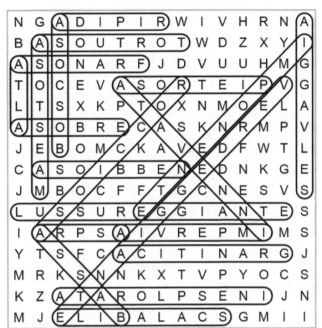

75a – Luci e ombre

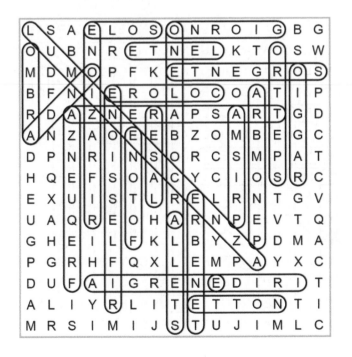

75b – Luci e ombre

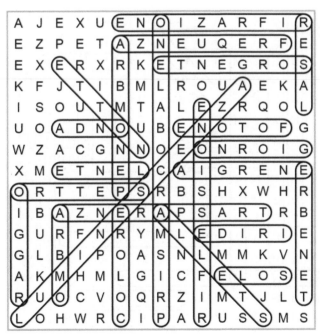

79 – Geografia dell'Italia

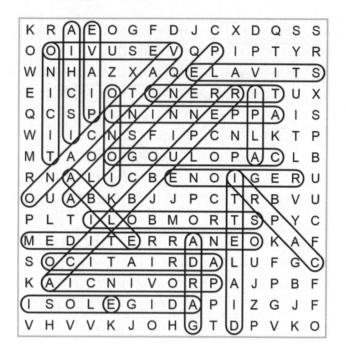

81a – I biomi

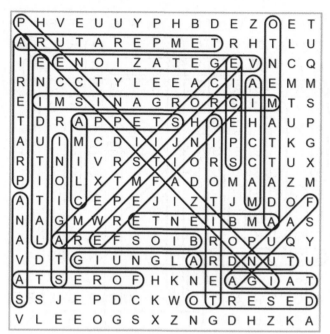

81b – I biomi

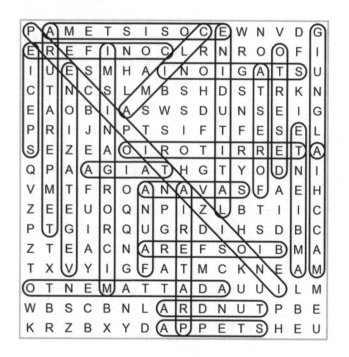

82a – Terremoti, tsunami e vulcani

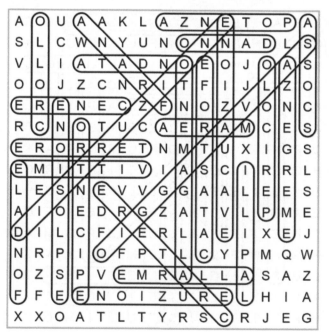

82b – Terremoti, tsunami e vulcani

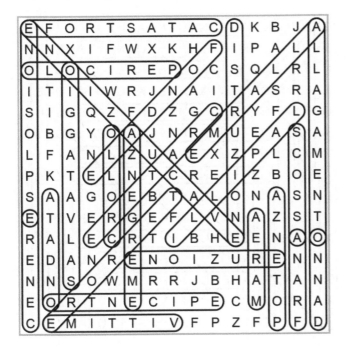

83a – Creature del mare e del fiume

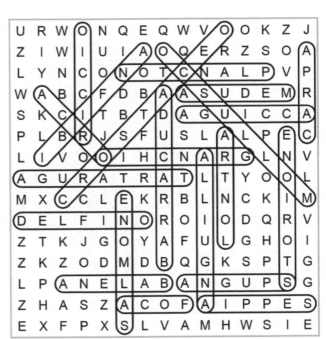

83b – Creature del mare e del fiume

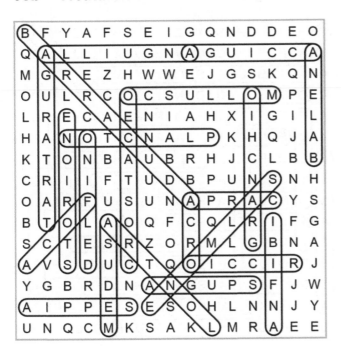

90a – Il mondo degli insetti

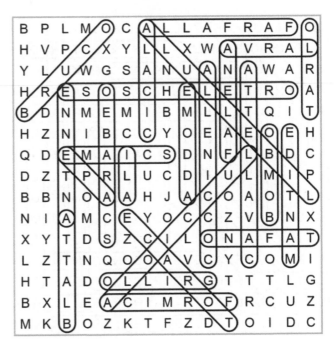

90b – Il mondo degli insetti

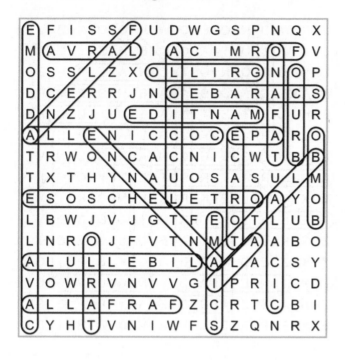

91a – Alcuni fiori

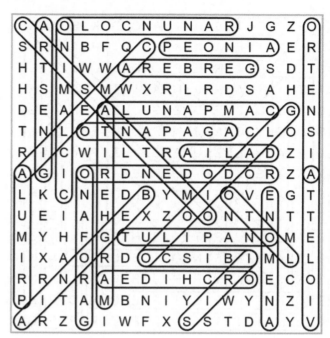

91b – Alcuni fiori

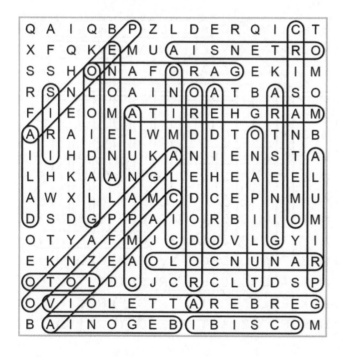

92a – Religioni del mondo e parole relative

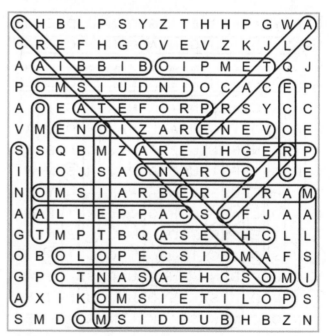

92b – Religioni del mondo e parole relative

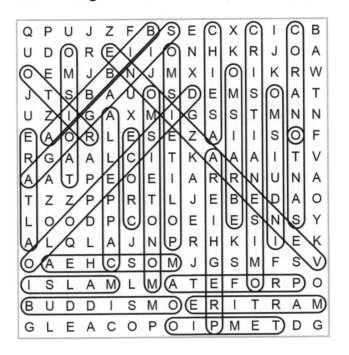

96a – Aggettivi del deserto

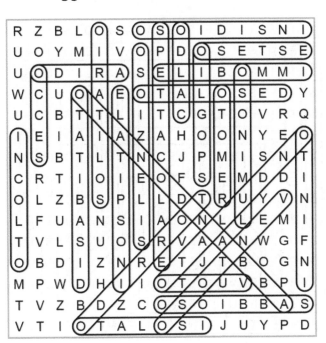

96b – Aggettivi del deserto

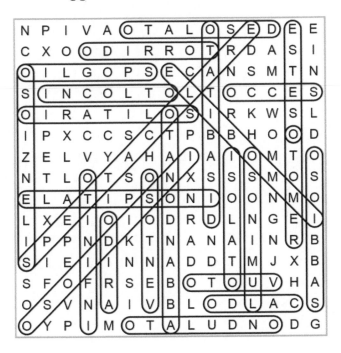

97a – Malattie infettive

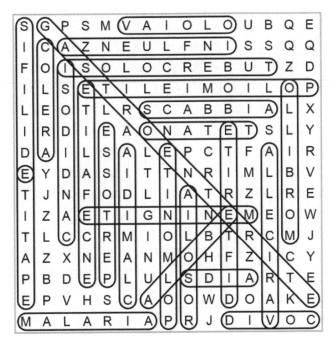

97b – Malattie infettive

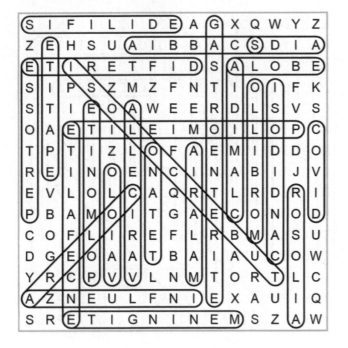

99a – Il mondo dell'agricoltura

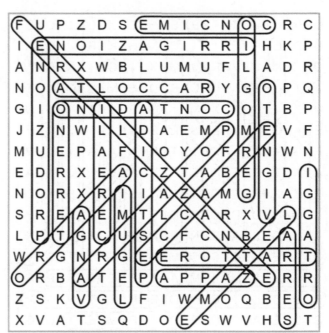

99b – Il mondo dell'agricoltura

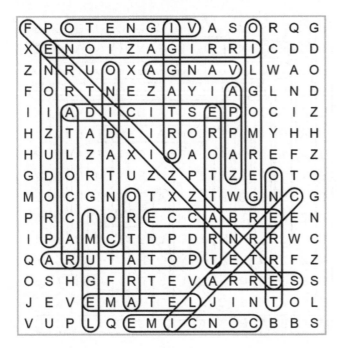

Freeform Crossword Solutions

3 – Insetti antipatici

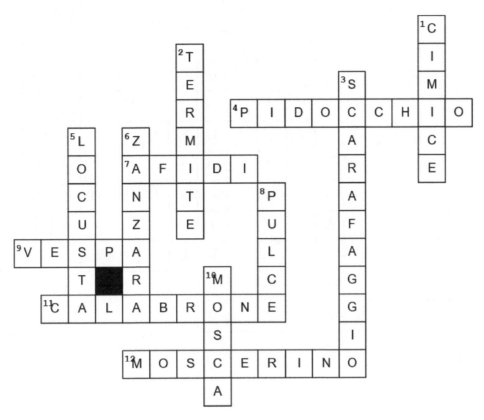

4 – Disastri naturali

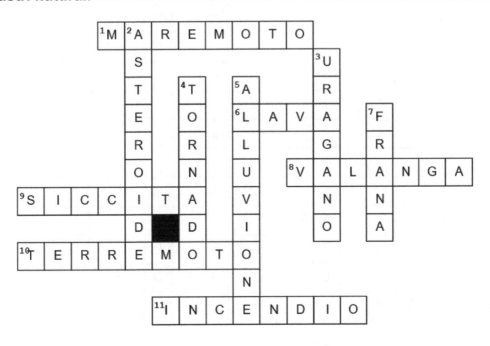

15 – Animali carnivori

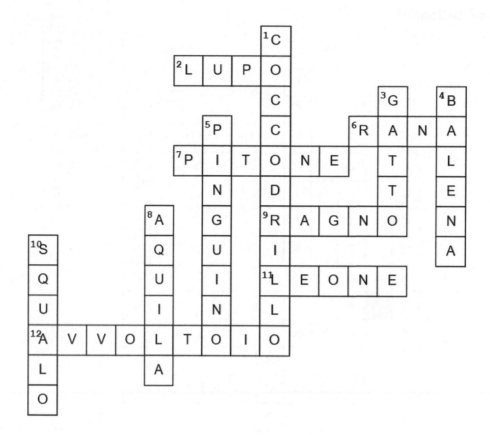

16 – Animali erbivori

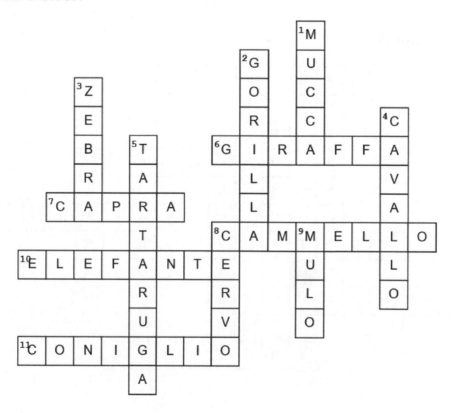

17 – Animali della fattoria

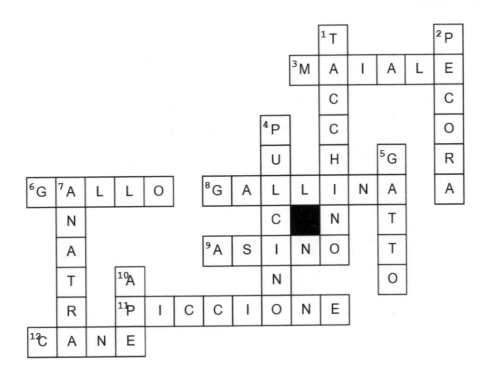

28 – Fiumi del mondo

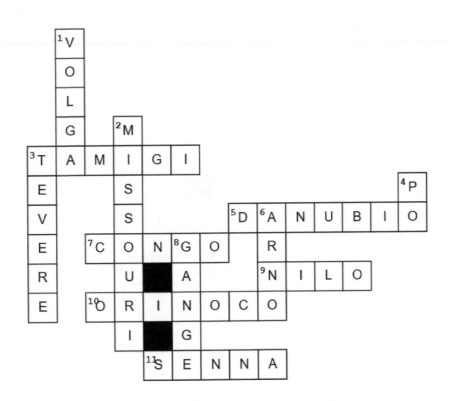

39 – Alcune capitali

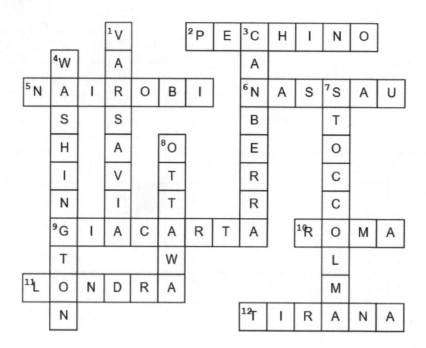

40 – Il pianeta Terra

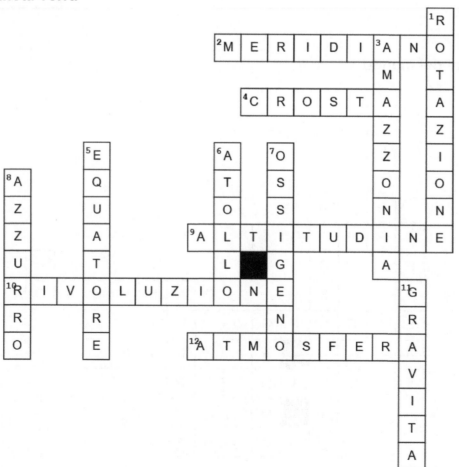

51 – Geografia dell'Italia

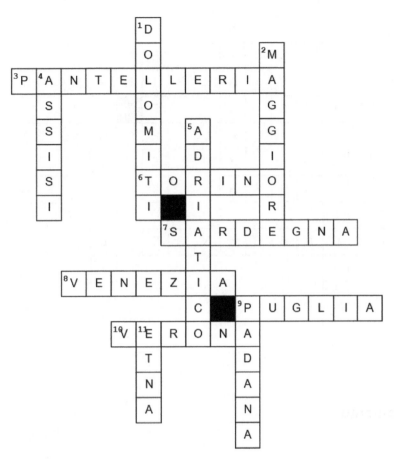

52 – Che tempo fa?

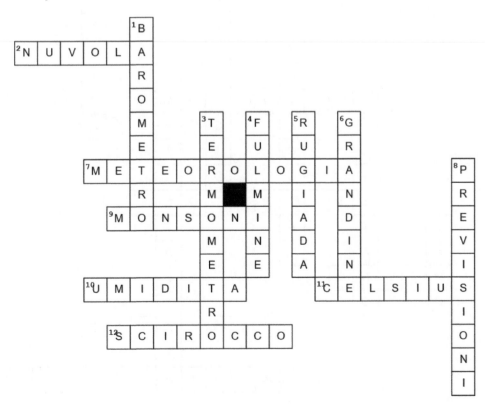

63 – Monumenti e luoghi spettacolari

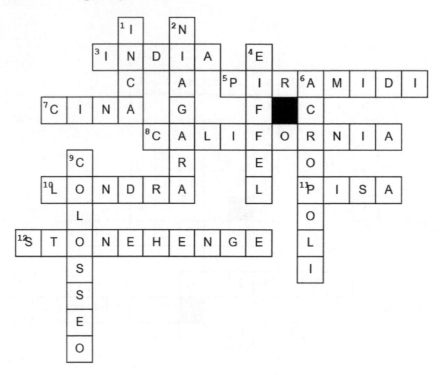

Across/Down (grid solution):
- 1. I
- 2. N
- 3. INDIA
- 4. E
- 5. PIR
- 6. AMIDI
- 7. CINA
- 8. CALIFORNIA
- 9. C
- 10. LONDRA
- 11. PISA
- 12. STONEHENGE

Grid letters (vertical):
- ICAGRA (from 1)
- NAGRA (from 2)
- EFELO (from 4)
- ACONIA (from 6)
- COLOSSEO (from 9)
- POLI (from 11)

64 – L'inquinamento

Grid solution:
- 1. PLASTICA
- 2. PES...
- 3. GHIACCI...
- 4. TRAFFICO
- 5. AMBIENTALI
- 6. RIFIUTI
- 7. METANO / ETA...
- 8. ESTINZIONE
- 9. SMOG
- 10. OZONO
- 11. TOSSICO
- 12. RADIAZIONI

76 – Continenti e oceani

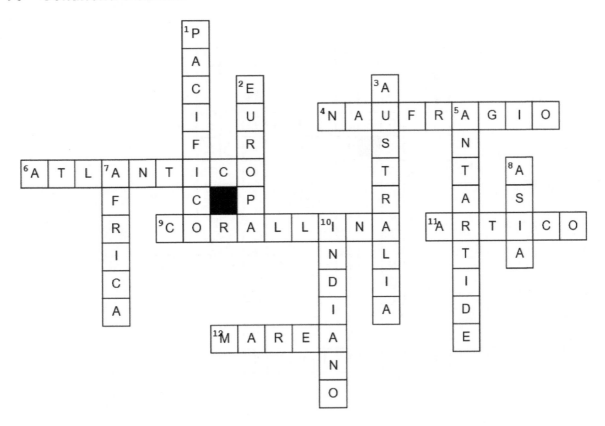

77 – Piante e fiori

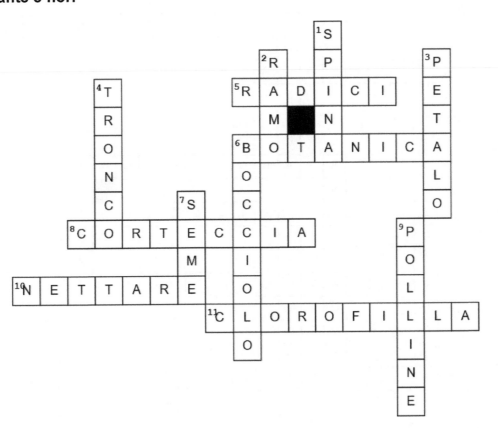

84 – Geografia del mondo

85 – Discipline scientifiche

94 – Animali invertebrati

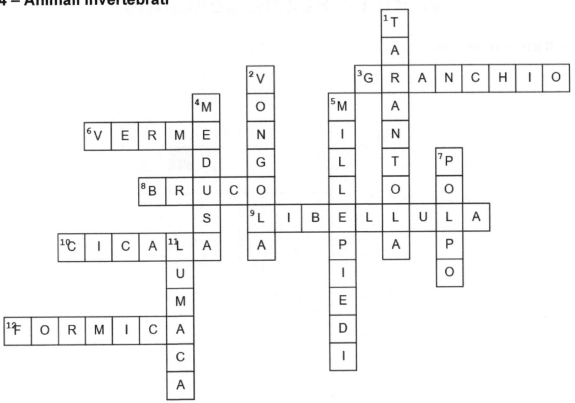

95 – Bandiere del mondo

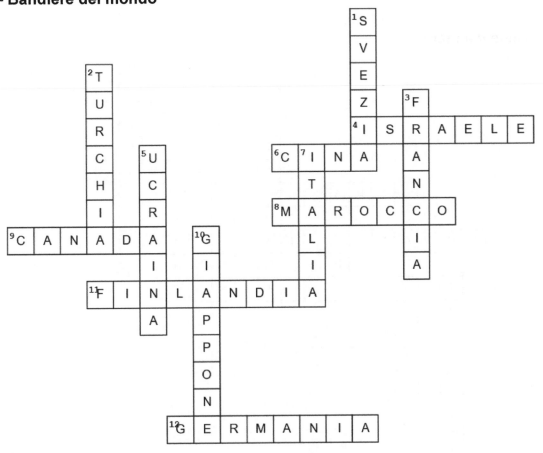

Word Fit Puzzle Solutions

7 – Il mondo dei felini

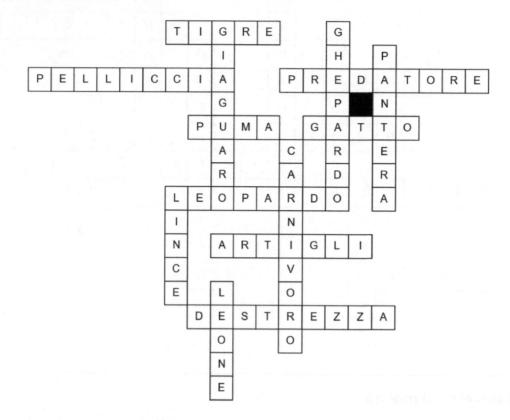

11 – Cose del mare

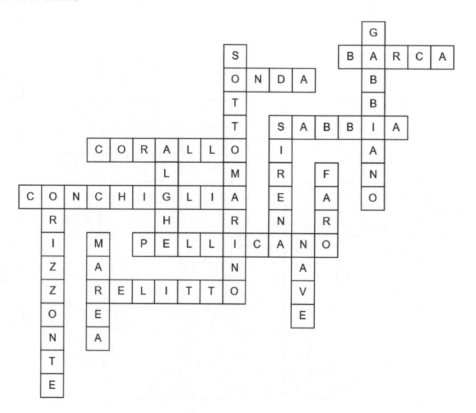

19 – Salviamo il pianeta

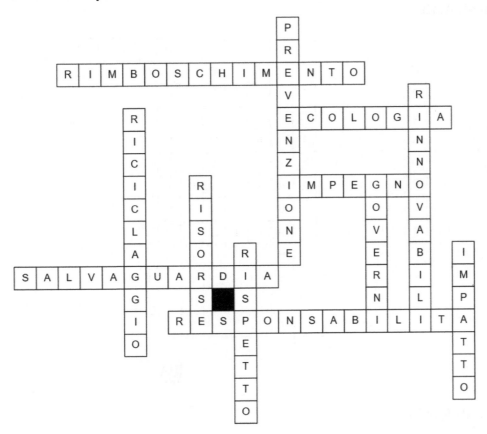

20 – Polo Nord e Polo Sud

31 – Fiori profumati

32 – In cerca di fossili

43 – Alcune civiltà

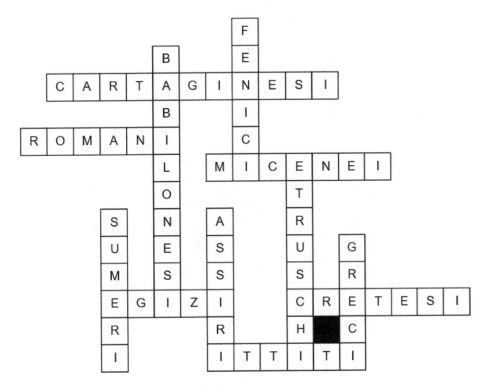

44 – La forza dei venti

55 – La cellula animale

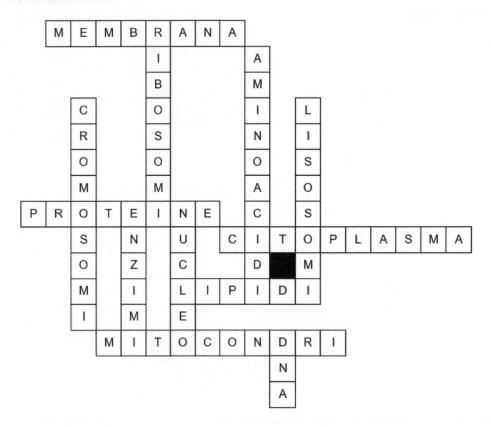

56 – I grandi esploratori

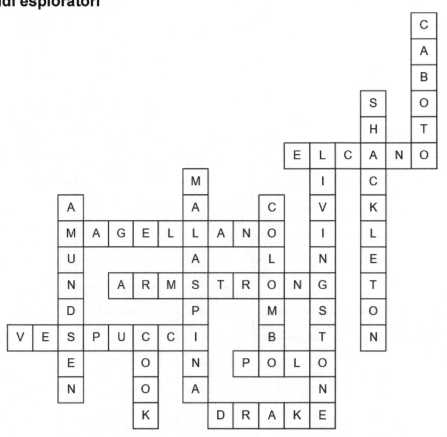

68 – Valute del mondo

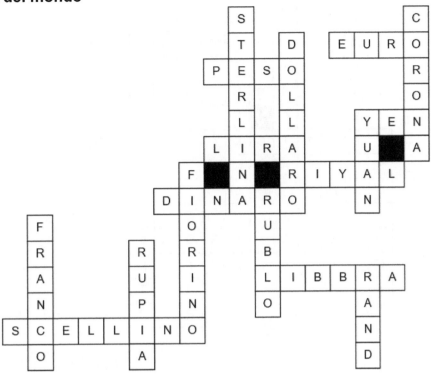

69 – La teoria dell'evoluzione

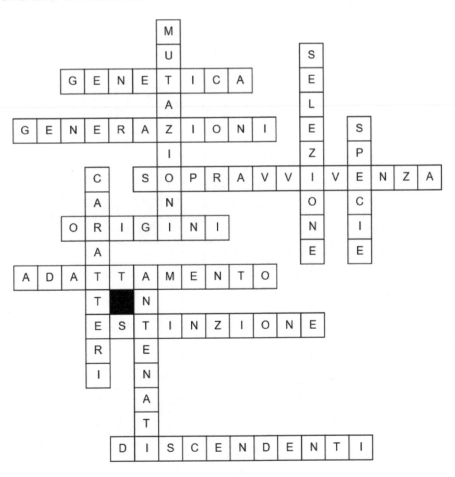

80 – L'atomo

88 – La crescita demografica

100 – In cerca di funghi

Word Match Solutions

5 – Uccelli rapaci

aquila	→	eagle
falco	→	hawk
nibbio	→	kite
avvoltoio	→	vulture
gufo	→	owl
condor	→	condor
gheppio	→	kestrel
poiana	→	buzzard
albanella	→	harrier
barbagianni	→	barn owl
sparviero	→	sparrowhawk
smeriglio	→	merlin

6 – Stagioni: inverno

pozzanghera	→	puddle
brina	→	frost
neve	→	snow
raffreddore	→	cold
buio	→	darkness
letargo	→	hybernation
freddo	→	cold
dicembre	→	December
arancia	→	orange
carciofo	→	artichoke
finocchio	→	fennel
abete	→	fir tree

17 – Animali che vanno in letargo

pipistrello	→	bat
orso	→	bear
ghiro	→	dormouse
bombo	→	bumblebee
rana	→	frog
scoiattolo	→	squirrel
riccio	→	hedgehog
lucertola	→	lizard
marmotta	→	marmot
procione	→	raccoon
serpente	→	snake
rospo	→	toad

18 – Stagioni: primavera

bocciolo	→	bud
agnello	→	lamb
nido	→	nest
germoglio	→	shoot
polline	→	pollen
risveglio	→	awakening
allergie	→	allergies
pulcino	→	chick
erba	→	grass
marzo	→	March
prato	→	meadow
farfalla	→	butterfly

29 – Suoni e natura

fiume	→	scorrere
foglie	→	frusciare
pioggia	→	scrosciare
fuoco	→	scoppiettare
fulmine	→	tuonare
uccelli	→	cinguettare
insetti	→	ronzare
cuore	→	battere
cavallo	→	galoppare
onda del mare	→	sciabordare
vento	→	soffiare
vulcano	→	eruttare

30 – Animali e cuccioli

mucca	→	vitello
cavallo	→	puledro
cervo	→	cerbiatto
gallina	→	pulcino
pecora	→	agnello
anatra	→	anatroccolo
aquila	→	aquilotto
volpe	→	volpacchiotto
capra	→	capretto
gatto	→	micetto
maiale	→	porcellino
orso	→	orsetto

41 – Stagioni: estate

caldo	→	heat
sole	→	sun
luce	→	light
girasole	→	sunflower
zanzara	→	mosquito
conchiglia	→	shell
granchio	→	crab
grillo	→	cricket
spiaggia	→	beach
giugno	→	June
albicocca	→	apricot
pesca	→	peach

42 – Piante medicinali

calendula	→	marigold
ortica	→	nettle
iperico	→	hypericum
zenzero	→	ginger
camomilla	→	chamomile
valeriana	→	valerian
peperoncino	→	chilli
curcuma	→	turmeric
lavanda	→	lavender
equiseto	→	horsetail
semi di lino	→	linseed
eucalipto	→	eucalyptus

53 – Animali e versi

leone	→	ruggisce
lupo	→	ulula
cinghiale	→	grugnisce
asino	→	raglia
elefante	→	barrisce
rana	→	gracida
scoiattolo	→	squittisce
anatra	→	starnazza
tacchino	→	gloglotta
serpente	→	sibila
piccione	→	tuba
cervo	→	bramisce

54 – Paesi e lingue ufficiali

San Marino	→	italiano
Algeria	→	arabo
Argentina	→	spagnolo
Austria	→	tedesco
Bangladesh	→	bengali
Barbados	→	inglese
Brasile	→	portoghese
Danimarca	→	danese
Grecia	→	greco
Israele	→	ebraico
Costa d'Avorio	→	francese
Iran	→	persiano

66 – Stagioni: autunno

raccolto	→	harvest
pioggia	→	rain
foglia	→	leaf
zucca	→	pumpkin
nebbia	→	fog
ghianda	→	acorn
castagna	→	chestnut
ragno	→	spider
fungo	→	mushroom
migrazione	→	migration
ottobre	→	October
nocciola	→	hazelnut

67 – Visitiamo le grotte

speleologo	→	speleologist
calcare	→	limestone
stalattite	→	stalactite
stalagmite	→	stalagmite
caverna	→	cavern
pozzo	→	well
sotterraneo	→	underground
erosione	→	erosion
galleria	→	tunnel
volta	→	vault
nicchia	→	recess
scavo	→	excavation

86 – Parti dell'albero e del frutto

tronco	→	trunk
radici	→	roots
foglie	→	leaves
rami	→	branches
chioma	→	crown
corteccia	→	bark
fiori	→	flowers
semi	→	seeds
picciolo	→	stalk
buccia	→	peel
polpa	→	pulp
torsolo	→	core

87 – Gli elementi chimici più abbondanti sulla terra

ossigeno	→	oxygen
silicio	→	silicon
alluminio	→	aluminium
ferro	→	iron
calcio	→	calcium
sodio	→	sodium
potassio	→	potassium
magnesio	→	magnesium
idrogeno	→	hydrogen
titanio	→	titanium
fosforo	→	phosphorus
manganese	→	manganese

Word Scramble Solutions

8a, 8b – Cose del deserto

ECMAOLML	→	CAMMELLO
POOICSENR	→	SCORPIONE
ABISAB	→	SABBIA
UAND	→	DUNA
AISO	→	OASI
ATUSCC	→	CACTUS
IZLNSOIE	→	SILENZIO
OAIRMGIG	→	MIRAGGIO
ETOVN	→	VENTO
EVELROP	→	POLVERE
STPAEMET	→	TEMPESTA
COAIRC	→	ROCCIA

23a, 23b – Erbe aromatiche

OAOLRL	→	ALLORO
OETAN	→	ANETO
ILACBOSI	→	BASILICO
DOAIROOCLN	→	CORIANDOLO
NOGCOLLAEDR	→	DRAGONCELLO
GAAMRAGONI	→	MAGGIORANA
NEMAT	→	MENTA
RGONOIA	→	ORIGANO
ZMOREOLPEZ	→	PREZZEMOLO
ARMOINSRO	→	ROSMARINO
AVAILS	→	SALVIA
OTIM	→	TIMO

35a, 35b – L'acqua in natura

ACSATCA	→	CASCATA
IFMUE	→	FIUME
GUANAL	→	LAGUNA
AEMR	→	MARE
COEAON	→	OCEANO
LPUAED	→	PALUDE
GAIPOGI	→	PIOGGIA
OZOZP	→	POZZO
OULLCESR	→	RUSCELLO
EEONGRST	→	SORGENTE
AGNSTO	→	STAGNO
ENRTETOR	→	TORRENTE

47a, 47b – Cose della giungla

IEFLC	→	FELCI
ELRAIB	→	ALBERI
AMISMCI	→	SCIMMIA
LPPPOAAGAL	→	PAPPAGALLO
ILLROAG	→	GORILLA
AAGOIUGR	→	GIAGUARO
OMRIFHEERIC	→	FORMICHIERE
IPARTO	→	TAPIRO
DNAOCAAN	→	ANACONDA
NACTOU	→	TUCANO
IAOPIGG	→	PIOGGIA
UISFC	→	FICUS

59a, 59b – Andiamo a caccia

RDPEA	→	PREDA
GGNASVAELI	→	SELVAGGINA
ULEICF	→	FUCILE
RTITOPLEIE	→	PROIETTILE
ARCAUTCIC	→	CARTUCCIA
RCAEFIC	→	FRECCIA
CAOR	→	ARCO
PARALOTP	→	TRAPPOLA
RMPNIAOT	→	IMPRONTA
OOCSB	→	BOSCO
PRASO	→	SPARO
NILOCOBO	→	BINOCOLO

65a, 65b – Andiamo a pescare

TREE	→	RETE
AABRC	→	BARCA
OAM	→	AMO
CSEA	→	ESCA
ZLAEN	→	LENZA
NANAC	→	CANNA
ELLUMNIOL	→	MULINELLO
AVILTIS	→	STIVALI
IDSAE	→	SEDIA
CSOECHI	→	SECCHIO
BAAL	→	ALBA
AEEIAGTGGNLL	→	GALLEGGIANTE

72a, 72b – Stati dell'America meridionale

TGNNIREAA	→	ARGENTINA
IAOVLIB	→	BOLIVIA
LSBRAEI	→	BRASILE
EICL	→	CILE
OICABLMO	→	COLOMBIA
UCDRAOE	→	ECUADOR
NYGAUA	→	GUYANA
AAYRUAPG	→	PARAGUAY
ÙRPE	→	PERÙ
MUNSREAI	→	SURINAME
GUUYUAR	→	URUGUAY
UVAENZLEE	→	VENEZUELA

78a, 78b – Cereali e derivati

EAANV	→	AVENA
ARFRO	→	FARRO
RFETNMOU	→	FRUMENTO
IASM	→	MAIS
IOGIML	→	MIGLIO
ROZO	→	ORZO
OSIR	→	RISO
EGSEAL	→	SEGALE
IARANF	→	FARINA
MDOAI	→	AMIDO
MSOLAE	→	SEMOLA
SACCUR	→	CRUSCA

89a, 89b – Animali ruminanti

ELAC	→	ALCE
LPIATENO	→	ANTILOPE
TAIREE	→	ARIETE
EOBTSNI	→	BISONTE
OBLUAF	→	BUFALO
AIOCCSOM	→	CAMOSCIO
ZLLAEZGA	→	GAZZELLA
AMALPI	→	IMPALA
NONEMTO	→	MONTONE
NMEOFUL	→	MUFLONE
ENNRA	→	RENNA
MSTOCACEB	→	STAMBECCO

93a, 93b – Alcuni Stati dell'Africa

EIGAALR	→	ALGERIA
GAALNO	→	ANGOLA
NBRUIUD	→	BURUNDI
MUCEARN	→	CAMERUN
IPATOEI	→	ETIOPIA
AAGIBM	→	GAMBIA
YNKEA	→	KENYA
UAAIARTNMI	→	MAURITANIA
CAORCOM	→	MAROCCO
CBMMOAZOI	→	MOZAMBICO
AIGIENR	→	NIGERIA
ATANNAZI	→	TANZANIA

98a, 98b – Il giorno e la notte

BAAL	→	ALBA
UORAAR	→	AURORA
UCLE	→	LUCE
OSEL	→	SOLE
TMTANIO	→	MATTINO
GIOPOEGRMI	→	POMERIGGIO
ASER	→	SERA
OTORTMAN	→	TRAMONTO
RUOCCULEPS	→	CREPUSCULO
OIUB	→	BUIO
AUNL	→	LUNA
ELSLET	→	STELLE

Cryptograms Solutions

9 – Quote by Ralph Waldo Emerson

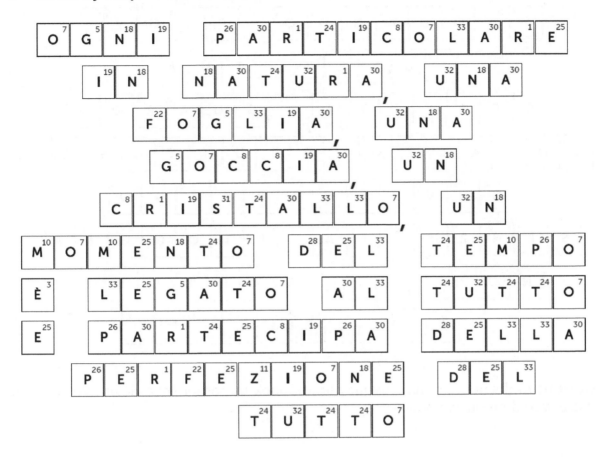

Translation: Every particular in nature, a leaf, a drop, a crystal, a moment of time is related to the whole, and partakes of the perfection of the whole.

---

10 – Quote by Cristoforo Colombo

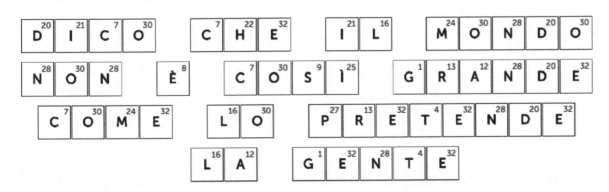

Translation: I say that the world is not as big as people make it out to be.

21 – Quote by G.K. Chesterton

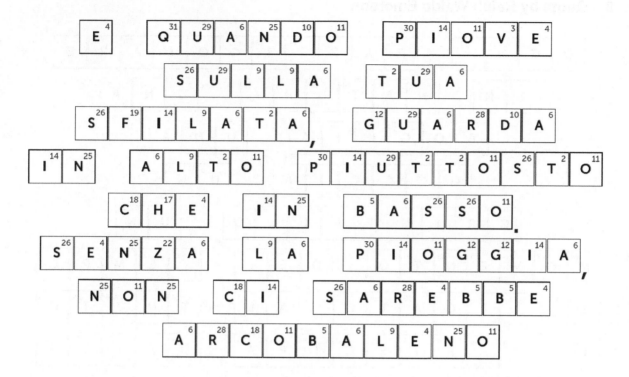

Translation: And when it rains on your parade, look up rather than down. Without the rain, there would be no rainbow.

---

22 – Quote by Marco Aurelio

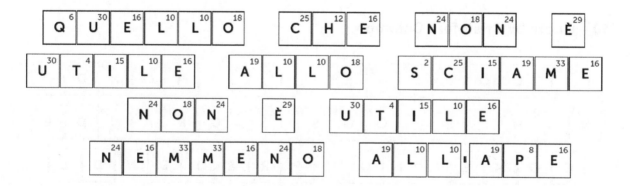

Translation: That which is not good for the swarm, neither is it good for the bee.

33 – Quote by Jules Verne

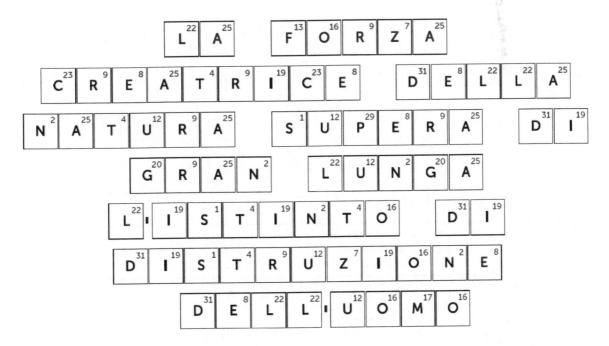

Translation: Nature's creative power is far beyond man's instinct of destruction.

---

34 – Quote by Galileo Galilei

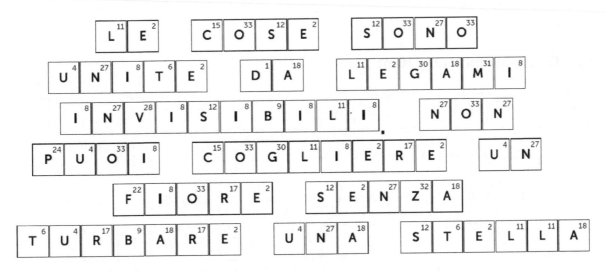

Translation: Things are united by invisible bonds. You cannot pick a flower without disturbing a star.

45 – Quote by Johann Wolfgang von Goethe

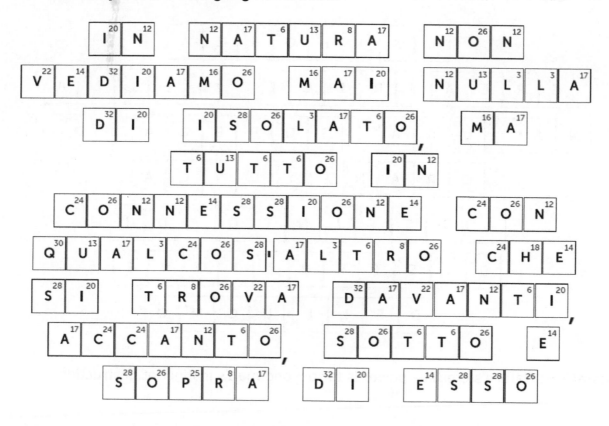

Translation: In nature we never see anything isolated, but everything in connection with something else which is before it, beside it, under it and over it.

---

46 – Quote by Immanuel Kant

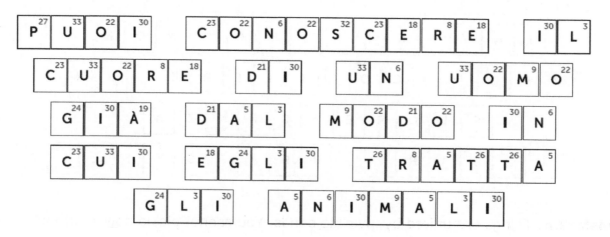

Translation: You can judge the heart of a man by his treatment of animals.

57 – Chinese proverb

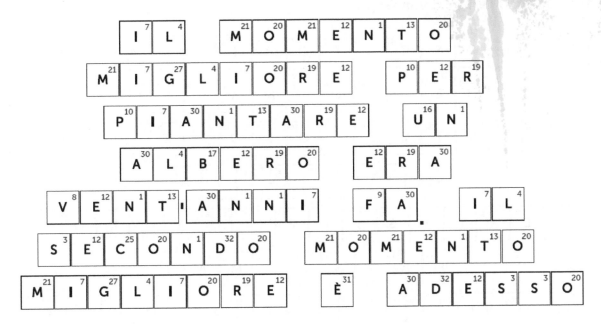

Translation: The best time to plant a tree was 20 years ago. The second best time is now.

58 – Quote by Michel de Montaigne

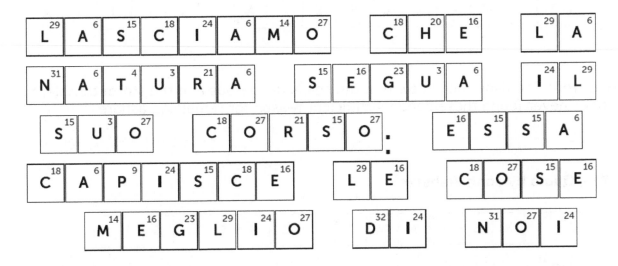

Translation: Let us permit nature to have her way. She understands her business better than we do.

70 – Quote by Vincent van Gogh

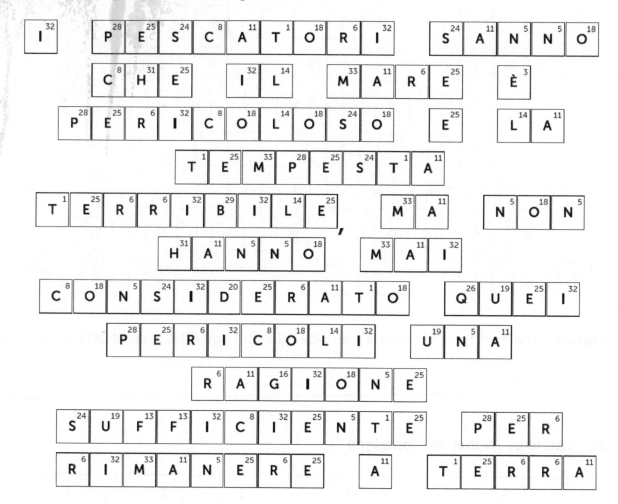

I PESCATORI SANNO
CHE IL MARE È
PERICOLOSO E LA
TEMPESTA
TERRIBILE, MA NON
HANNO MAI
CONSIDERATO QUEI
PERICOLI UNA
RAGIONE
SUFFICIENTE PER
RIMANERE A TERRA

Translation: The fishermen know that the sea is dangerous and the storm terrible, but they have never found these dangers sufficient reason for remaining ashore.

---

71 – Quote by John Webster

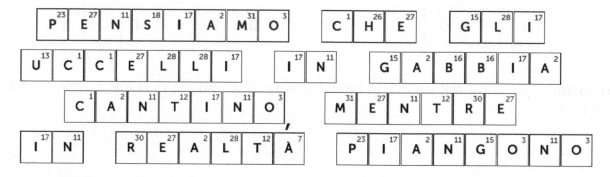

PENSIAMO CHE GLI
UCCELLI IN GABBIA
CANTINO MENTRE
IN REALTÀ PIANGONO

Translation: We think caged birds sing, when indeed they cry.